WHALE NATION

WHALE
NATION

Heathcote Williams

JONATHAN CAPE
THIRTY-TWO BEDFORD SQUARE LONDON

'Oceanos, the genesis of all . . .'
Homer, *The Iliad*, bk14, l.246

Contents

'Leviathan...
Upon earth there is not his like,
   who is made without fear.
Will he speak soft words unto thee?'

Job 41

From space, the planet is blue.
From space, the planet is the territory
Not of humans, but of the whale.

Blue seas cover seven-tenths of the earth's surface,
And are the domain of the largest brain ever created,
With a fifty-million-year-old smile.

Ancient, unknown mammals left the land
In search of food or sanctuary,
And walked into the water.

Their arms and hands changed into water-wings;

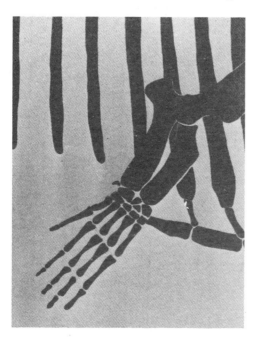

Their tails turned into boomerang-shaped tail-flukes,
Enabling them to fly, almost weightless, through the oceans;
Their hind-legs disappeared, buried deep within their flanks.

Free from land-based pressures:
Free from droughts, earthquakes, ice-ages, volcanoes, famine,
Larger brains evolved, ten times as old as man's . . .
Other creatures, with a larger cerebral cortex,
Luxuriantly folded, intricately fissured,
Deep down, in another country,
Moving at a different tempo.

And the whale's lips formed their distant, humorous curl,
When we were clawed quadrupeds,
Insect-eating shrews,
Feverishly scrabbling at the bark of trees.

*'...this great and wide sea, wherein...there is that
Leviathan, whom Thou hast made to play therein.'*
                                          Psalm 104: 26

Whales play, in an amniotic paradise.
Their light minds shaped by buoyancy, unrestricted by gravity,
Somersaulting,
Like angels, or birds;
Like our own lives, in the womb.

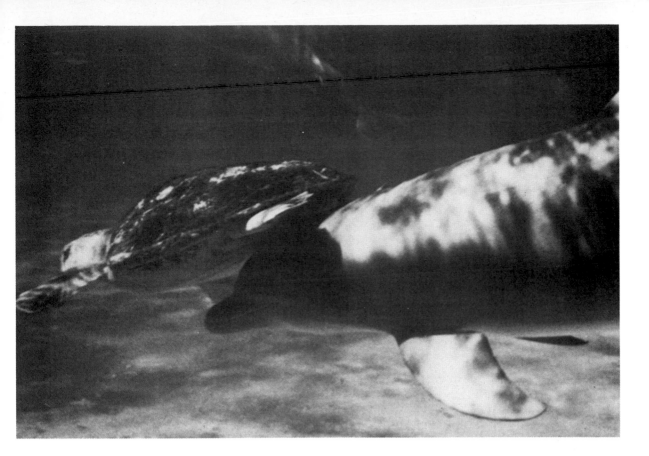

Whales play
For three times as long as they spend searching for food:
Delicate, involved games,
With floating seabirds' feathers, blown high into the air,
And logs of wood
Flipped from the tops of their heads;
Carried in their teeth
For a game of tag, ranging across the entire Pacific.
Play without goals.

Naked,
With skin like oiled silk,
Smooth as glass,
They move at fifty miles an hour.
Attaining faultless streamlining
By subtly changing the shape of their bodies:
Altering ridges of cartilage, and indentations of flesh
To correspond to constantly differing patterns of water;
To accommodate minute oscillations with vibrant inflexions of
    muscle and skin,
So that layers of liquid glide over each other,
In an easy, laminar flow.
No drag, no turbulence.
A velvet energy.

Like Buddhists,
They are not compulsive eaters.
They can go for eight months without food;
And they do not work to eat.
They play to eat.

The Humpback catches its food by blowing bubbles.
Five-foot-wide bubbles, as large as weather-balloons:
When they burst, they make a circle of confusing mist.

The plankton: the Arctic shrimps, the krill, the sea-butterflies
Are corralled into the middle by a bewildering ring of hissing
   bubble-bombs.

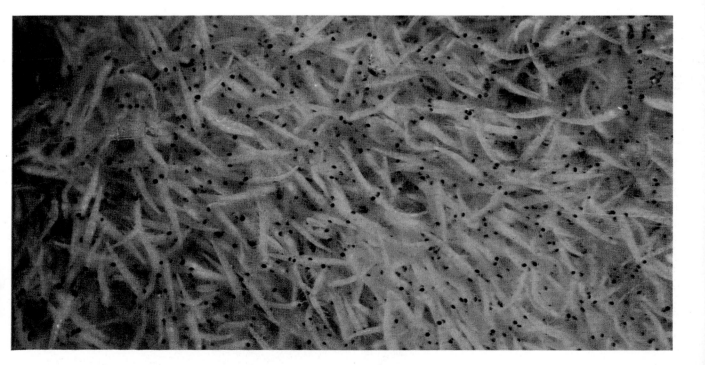

The whale then rises up
Into the centre of a round plate of brimming water,
And eats.

. . . Imagine blowing soap-bubbles,
And food drops out of the sky.

After dinner, music:
Ethereal music that carries for miles,
A siren's song,
Leading sailors to believe,
As the sounds infiltrated through the wooden hull,
That their vessels were haunted
By spirits of the deep.

Webs of elegant cetacean music stretch around the globe;
Lyrical litanies on the bio-radio
That draw on an oral tradition of submarine songs
From a living memory bank, founded fifty million years ago.

Different dialects; different themes;
Different clusters of notes, sequences, phrases, sub-phrases,
Sung with different cadences and modulations
To send different messages
To different individuals.
Different songs from day to day, from year to year:
An indication that there are creatures, other than man, still
    evolving.

Millions of mysterious sounds memorised
And passed on from generation to generation;
All clearly retained in the mind
Uncluttered by cuneiform tablets, vellum, paper, newsprint,
    floppy discs...
Free of all methods of transcription
Which, disconnected from the body-language of the informant,
Facilitate deceit.

Alien beings.
Their whole body: every bone, every membrane, every hollow,
Part of an enormous ear,
Twenty times as sensitive as man's.

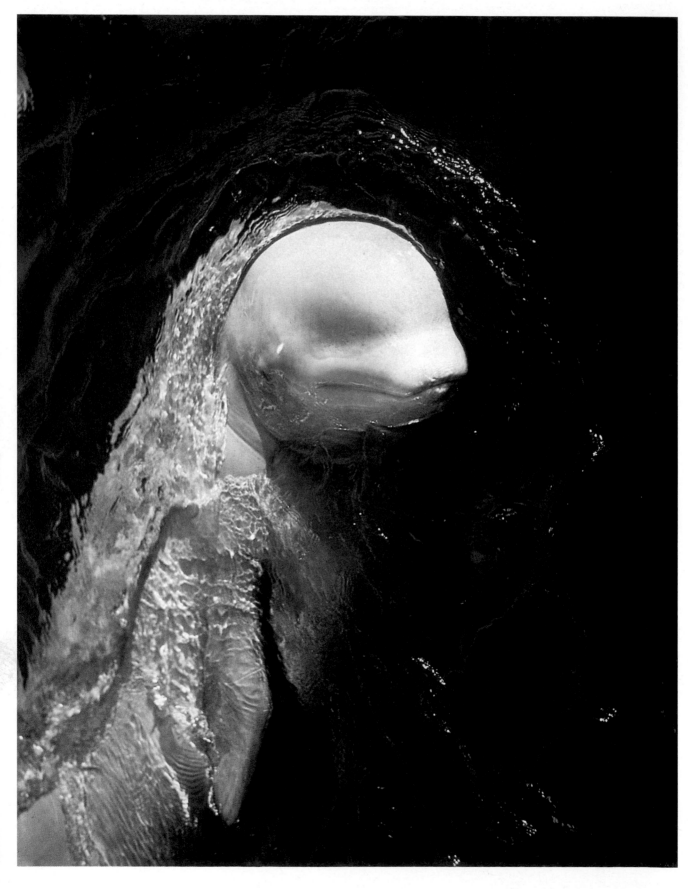

Whale families, whale tribes,
All have different songs:
An acoustic picture-language,
Spirited pulses relayed through water
At five times the speed sound travels through air,
Varied enough to express complex emotions,
Cultural details,
History,
News,
A sense of the unknown.
A lone Humpback may put on a solo concert lasting for days.
Within a Humpback's half-hour song
There are a hundred million bytes.
A million changes of frequency,
And a million tonal twists . . .

An Odyssey, as information-packed as Homer's,
Can be told in thirty minutes;
Fifty-million-year-old sagas of continuous whale mind:

Accounts of the forces of nature;
The minutiae of a shared consciousness;
Whale dreams;

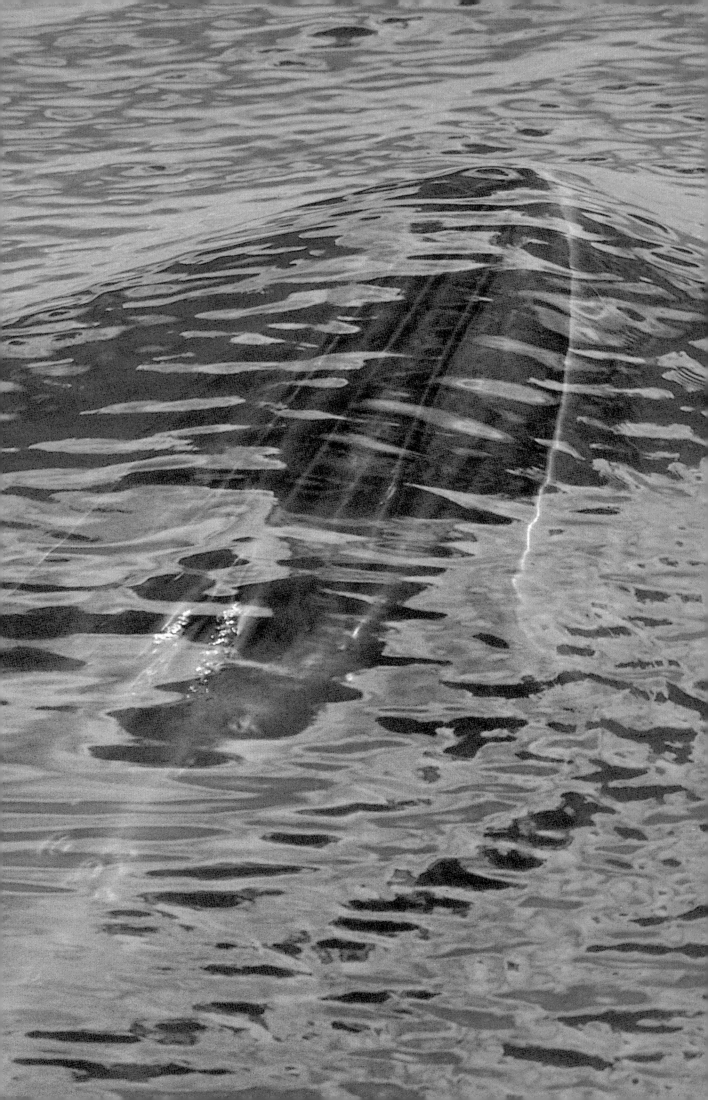

The accumulated knowledge of the past;

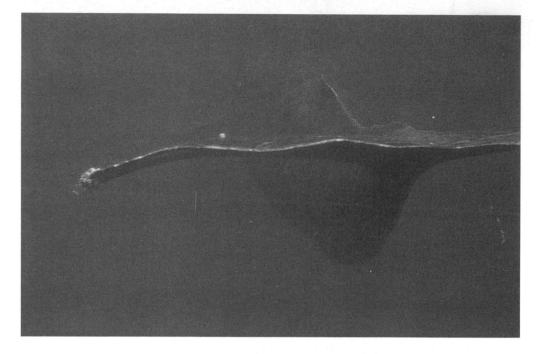

Rumours of ancestors, the Archaeoceti,
With life-spans of two and three hundred years;

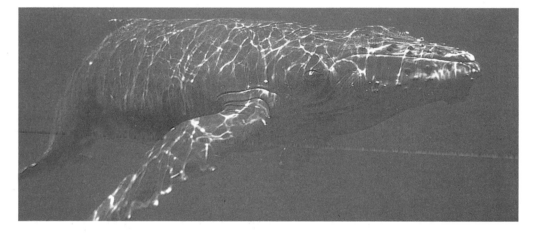

Memories of loss;
Memories of ideal love;
Memories of meetings . . .

For the Rorqual whales,
Into whose mouths fourteen people could be placed with
    headroom,
Hold meetings,
In certain places, set aside, near the breeding lagoons.

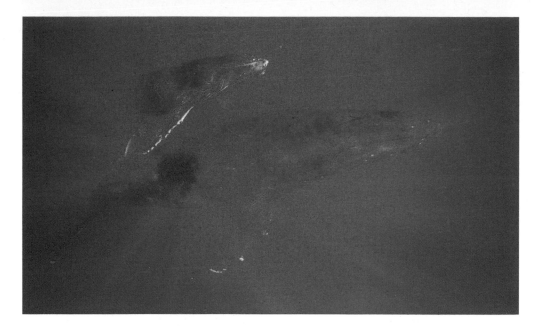

Evenly spaced, in a watery stadium,
They stand, vertically, like megaliths.
A third of their bodies above the surface,
Rhythmically threshing the water beneath them;
Breathing in unison;
Cliffs of flesh, their heads quite still,
Talking in ultrasound,
Followed by long, superhuman silences
As if in a collective reverie: their brains off-line, updating their
    programmes;
Their brains six times the size of man's,
With a large area of silent parietal and frontal lobe,
Like man's,
For assessing the past
And forecasting the future.

Their antique, crusty heads
Are festooned with regal tassels of vegetation:
Thick, dangling fronds and swatches of Sargasso seaweed
Hang off their stalked acorn-barnacles.

They stand, eerily,
Like benign, long-suffering ghouls;
Animated standing-stones,
Exchanging information with high resolution,
Detecting sounds a microsecond long.
Unearthly creatures inhabiting a medium eight hundred times
    denser than air.

The whale moves in a sea of sound:
Shrimps snap, plankton seethes,
Fish croak, gulp, drum their air-bladders,
And are scrutinised by echo-location,
A light massage of sound
Touching the skin.

The small, toothed whales use high frequencies:
Finely tuned and focused sound-beams,
Intense salvoes of bouncing clicks, a thousand a second,
With which a hair, as thin as half a millimetre, can be detected;
Penetrating probes,
With which they can scan the contents of a colleague's stomach,
Follow the flow of their blood,
Take the full measure of an approaching brain.

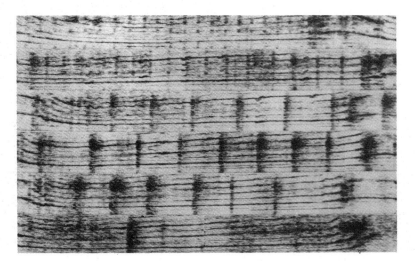

From two cerebral cavities in their melon-shaped heads,
They can transmit two sonic probes, as if talking in stereo,
And send them in any direction at the same time:
One ahead, one behind, one above, one below...
Lengthening the sound-waves, shortening them, heightening
   them,
Until their acoustic switchboard receives the intelligence
   required.

Spoken to in English,
The smallest cetacean, the dolphin,
Will rise to the surface,
Alter its vocal frequencies to suit the measures of human
   speech,
Pitch its voice to the same level as that of human sounds
When travelling through air – an unfamiliar medium –
Adjust the elastic lips of its blow-hole,
And then, after courteously waiting for silence,
Produce a vibrato imitation of human language:
Words, phrases, sentences...

Cybernetic attempts to mimic delphinese
Meet with a pained snort of disappointment,
Followed by a deep dive to a place of refuge,
Where the ratcheting, metallic ticks are less audible.

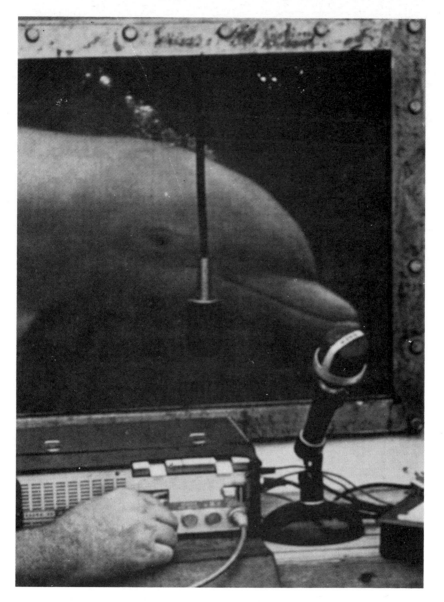

The larger whales use lower frequencies,
At greater depths, rumbling like generators,
Wavering, trans-oceanic throbs,
With which they keep in contact with their tribe, over
    hundreds of miles,
Building up accurate echo-pictures of their positions in the sea,
And detecting giant squids, thirty-five feet long,
Krakens, concealed in pitch-black grottoes.

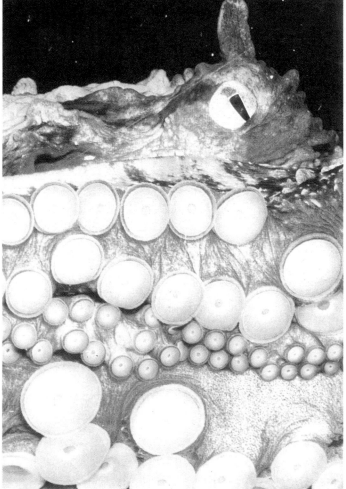

The Blue whale is nearly a hundred feet long.
It weighs a hundred and seventy tons,
As much as two thousand seven hundred people.
Its tongue is ten feet thick, heavier than an elephant.
It has seven stomachs.
Arteries you could swim through.
A half-ton heart, and eight tons of blood.

It has seven-gallon testicles.
It eats a million calories a day.
It has as many living cells within its body
As there are people in the world.
It lives for a hundred and twenty years.
A dark blue nucleus in the transparent plasma of the sea.

. . . . A gargantuan heart at the hub of things:
For the baleen whales superintend the earth's largest bio-mass,
Plankton,
From which almost all the oxygen in the world derives.

They spend their lives amongst it,
Farming vast drifts, luminous meadows of plankton,
The central atoms of life.
Serious creatures, performing a serious task;
Slate-blue immensities, individually marbled;
Power-houses, in charge of the world's breath.

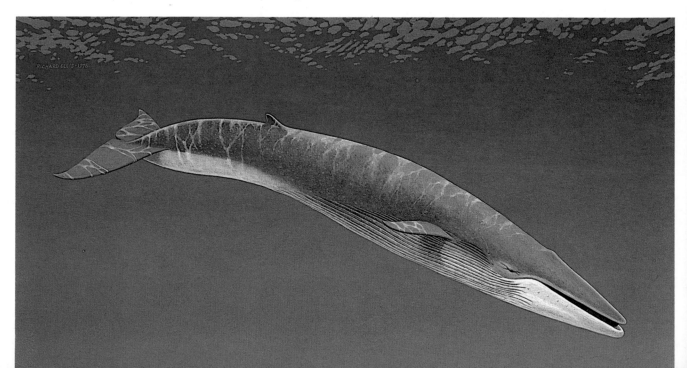

For without their attentions,
With their grazing-pressure removed,
The oxygen-producing plankton would breed uncontrollably,
Fractionally raise the temperature of the ocean,
Overheat their habitat,
Destroy the air-conditioned equilibrium of their global
    crucible,
And die . . .
Their wan blue light fading,
Taking this atmosphere with it,
Like a dying man, sucking his last breath through his teeth,
Leaving the ocean basins filled with a thick, dead broth . . .
Strangely echoing the former belief in *Bahamut*
A fabulous whale who provided the base
Upon which the whole world rested.

. . . And from its pre-historic, main-frame mind,
From its head, twenty-five feet in length,
The Blue whale,
The largest creature ever to have lived upon this planet,
Now and again utters an ominous whistle
Of a hundred and eighty-eight decibels . . .
Louder than Concorde.

Without hands, for making external tools,

Without depending on tons upon tons of artefacts, destined as
    litter,
The whale's sophistication has become internal:

Its skills are all perceptive,
Social, sensual, jokey,
Non-manipulative.

With their skilful acoustic sense,
Outstripping their eyesight,
They may have developed vision...

When whales breed,
They breed with ecological consideration:
They breed in precise relation to the amount of food in the sea.

After a season foraging under the Arctic ice-floes,

Through which the Narwhal has made breathing holes
With its unicorn horn, for the use of all species,
The baleen whales leave their pinnacled ice-palaces,

And find their way south, to mate.
With glowing tracks behind them in the water, large as ships',
The Humpbacks use the rotational forces of the planet,
The azimuth of the sun,
The taste and temperature of the tides,
The contours of the sea-bed:
Canyons, plains, vaults;
The mountainous summits of the mid-Atlantic ridge, twice the
    width of the Andes,
Which stretches for ten thousand miles, from Iceland to
    Patagonia;
Guided by hydrothermal vents in the earth's crust,
The topography of coral reefs,
The position of the moon, and its tidal pull;
Navigating with a lodestone disc made of polarised magnetite,
A compass in the brain,
Sensitive to the geomagnetic flow of force-fields
Under phosphorescent seas,
They find their way to the mating grounds.

On arriving at their liquid seraglio,
Sealed off from the outside world by riptides,
Success in courtship is determined by whoever sings the most
   absorbing song.
And whoever makes the wildest movements with their body;
Knifing through foam
Spinning and wave-riding,

Spy-hopping, lob-tailing,
Breaching and tail-slapping;
Turning upside-down

And thwacking their bat-like flukes against the surface
With sharp, echoing cracks;
Throwing themselves into odd, alluring shapes;

Sinuously whirling and flickering through the sea

They glide past each other,
Swishing contemplatively,
Testing congenial feelings,
Judging the suppleness of motion,
Judging sensation, with gentle discrimination.

Mutual attraction is an elaborate, thoughtful process:
In whales the male member is erected voluntarily,
Unsheathed from within deep abdominal folds,
Erected, and then collapsed and concealed again, by an act of
    will –
Unlike in man,
Where it has an unseasonal, disconnected life of its own.
...And the Blue whale's penis is nine feet long,
Which may require additional self-control.

The two whales draw closer,
Fanning each other,
Then stroking each other with their pectoral fins.
Giant pink genital lips roll back underneath the water.

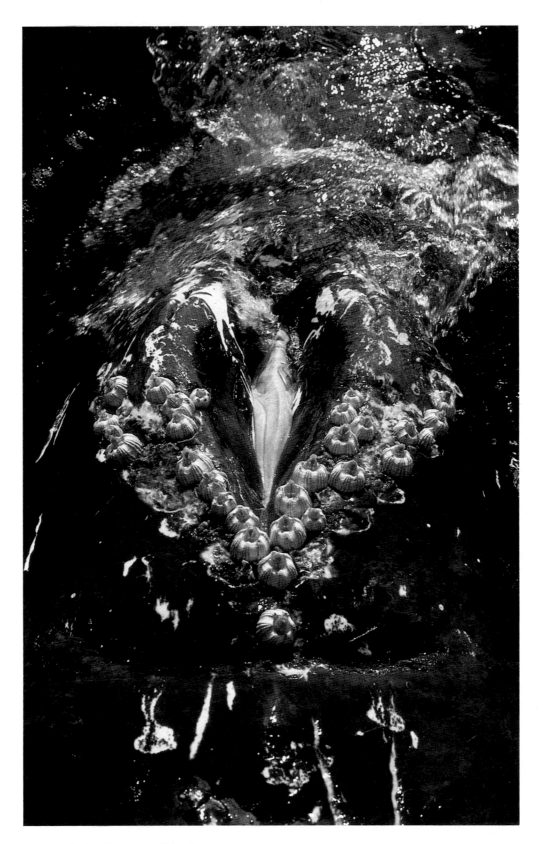

They join forces. Embrace.
Mating face to face, like man.

Stirring their huge tail-flukes,
Their heads emerge slowly above the water.
They clutch each other, their long flippers around each other,
The accordion pleats of their grooved bellies interleave,
They move their flukes backwards and forwards beneath them,
Their bodies are pressed closer and closer,
As they drive themselves upwards,
Rising out of the sea,
Out of the shimmering green shadows below,
Into the exhilarating glare of the sky.
With a last movement,
Powerfully churning their flukes in unison, fifty feet below,
They propel themselves upwards,
Gallons of water sluicing down their sides,
They both jump clear,
Held together, in mid-air, for their massive climax.

The sea moves,
And any earthly thing near by is swamped.

They dive.
Curving their bodies, they dive a mile down.
Dropping their heart-beat,
Collapsing their lungs,
Folding in their ribs along articulated joints, to counteract the
    bends,
Happily slipping through the pressure of five hundred
    atmospheres,
A quarter of a million tons of dense water at the sea-bed,
Exerted on their bodies.

Half an hour, an hour later,
They emerge,
Triumphantly blowing like blast furnaces.
Three thousand times the contents of the human lung
Is expelled in two seconds through their air-pipes,
In a great sigh of steam.

Plumes of warm mist, twenty feet high,
Jet from their blow-holes; exuberant exclamation marks
    punctuating the sky.
Their spouting exhalations are audible for half a mile,
Sounding like distant thunder,
And looking like puffs of chimney smoke
From an underwater town.

They inhale.
As the air enters the endless corridors of their bodies,
It gives off the sound of a reverberating bell.

Eleven months later,
The first sound a whale calf hears
Is singing.
The mother lifts her new-born calf to the surface,
And then rolls on to her side,
Expressing her milk into its mouth with muscles deep inside
    her breasts:
Twice as rich in protein as human milk,
Richer than clotted cream.

The songs of their escorts
Filter through the water,
The element of baptism,
In which the whale calf is to be perennially immersed.

Should anything untimely happen to it,
Its mother will support her calf upon her back
Until it disintegrates.

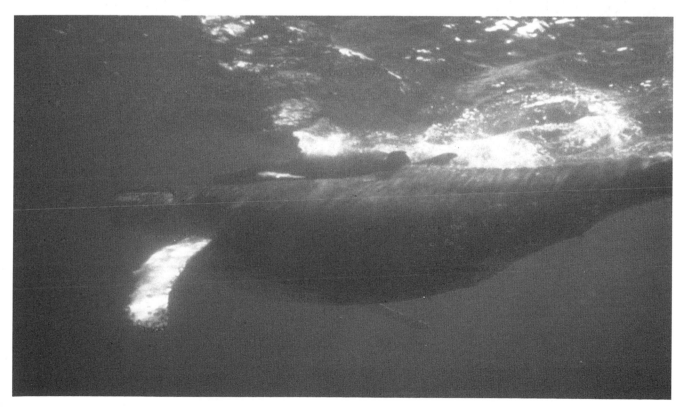

The Inuit say: 'We like the way whales think,'
And 'the whale is good to imagine.'

The Kwakiutl of Alert Bay
Believe that the whale is 'a long-life maker'
Who brings prosperity.

The Nootka claim that the whale allows his death,
To spare people from hunger,
And that therefore they must be worthy of it.

But other men have elected to view the whale
As an essential component of an expanding economy . . .

When an underwater shape is detected on the submarine radar,
Catcher boats are despatched from the factory-ship.
The harpoon on the raised foredeck is manned
And swivelled in the direction of the whale.

As the whale comes within range,
The engine's screw is slowed down,
And then silenced.

An accurate shot lands between the shoulder-blades.
An inaccurate shot is followed up by two, three or four more.

At the end of the five-foot-long steel harpoon
A small serrated cup prevents ricochet.

The tip strikes,
Followed by a time-fused charge exploding three seconds later,
Splintering and lacerating the harpoon's way into the whale's side.

Next to the grenade,
Four barbed flanges pivot on hinges,
And as the whale struggles,
The strain on the rope snaps the barbs open:
They fly out, ripping into the lungs and inner organs,
Embedding the harpoon inside the whale,
Anchoring her body.

The whale clashes her jaws together,
Pants, flurries, and spurts blood raspingly through her
    blow-hole.
She thrashes her tail against the surface,
Strenuously heaving at the six-inch-thick nylon line
Attached to accumulator springs in the catcher-boat's hold,
Designed to buffer every move.

Twenty minutes pass.
The whale's ribs become too heavy to move.
The whale's rib muscles give up their strength.
The air-valves collapse, admitting a rush of sea-water;
The whale's lungs flood.
She suffocates and dies,
Revolving slowly in the water
Leaving her white stomach exposed.

A hollow lance,
Attached to an air-line,
Is fired at her upturned belly,
Feeding compressed air into her corpse,
To inflate it and keep it afloat.

An identifying flag –
With a radar reflector and the catcher-boat's number –
Is lobbed into her.

She is left to drift,
Rimmed with oil-slick and blood.

With no enemies in the sea
The whale is loth to believe in the attack,
As were the Indians, as were the aborigines.

The factory-ship, large as an aircraft carrier,
With the capacity to deal with a whale every thirty minutes,
Draws alongside.

A hole is bored into the nearest end of her body, lips or tail.
A tow-line is attached,
And she is hauled to the bottom of the ramp.

A set of moving claws is lowered towards her.
The hawser wire is pulled.
The curved fingers of the metal tongs bite.

The whale is inched up the slope on to the flensing deck.

Wearing spiked plates on their boots to pin themselves to the body,
The flensing crew, armed with long-handled knives,
Slice into the whale,
Scoring huge straps, eighteen inches wide and ten feet long;

Wires are looped around the ends of the loose flesh,
And winches tear it from the whale's side.

The whale is stuffed through manholes,
To be carved into a sodden mess by whirring knives
That lie below in rotating drums.

The minced flesh is shunted into digester-tanks
And boiled down for four hours by super-heated steam.
The solid residue is dried and bagged up.
The oil is piped into the separator house:
Double-boiled, centrifuged,
Hardened into edible fats,
Graded into half a dozen categories,
Barrelled and stored.

On deck, the skull, jaw-bones, ribs, spine and pelvis
Are dismembered with chain-saws,
Then ground down, and shovelled into the bone-cookers;
Melted and milled into chicken-feed and fertilisers.

From a whale who was pregnant,
The unborn are dragged into the meat-boilers
With huge hooks slung into their blow-holes.

The inner organs are towed into other boilers
To be distilled into pharmaceuticals.
The skin is collected from the slipways for glycerine.
The belly blubber is reserved for a delicacy known as 'whale
   bacon'.
The jaw cartilage is pickled.
The tail-flukes are frozen, to be eaten raw.

The floating factory has done little but exchange twenty
   thousand gallons of petroleum
For twenty thousand gallons of animal oil.
Foreign currency has been acquired.
The odd fact that no whale has been found with a serious
   pathological disease,
No whale has ever been found suffering from cancerous
   tumours,
Is overlooked.

Yet civilisation was built on the back of the whale:
Coastal settlements followed the presence of whales;
Shore-stations near the whaling grounds became cities.

Boston, New York, Plymouth,
Tokyo, Leningrad, Vladivostok,
Lisbon, Bergen, Brest,
Odessa, Yokohama, San Francisco,
Reykjavik, Valdivia, San Pedro,
Vancouver, Sydney, Durban,
Rotterdam, Whitby, Hull,
Darwin, Buenos Aires, Hobart,
Wellington, Auckland, Helsinki,
Seoul, Murmansk, Manila,
Valparaiso, Glasgow, Dundee,
Philadelphia, Liverpool...

London, Hamburg...

Urban conglomerations plugged into the corpse of the whale,
Growing larger and larger by its light.

The whale's insulating wet-suits hacked off in flensing ships
In untold billions:

For fuel;

For lamps
And candlewax, to turn night into day;

For whale-oil appliances for sweat-shops,
And factories;

For domestic lighting;
For street lighting;
For shop lighting;

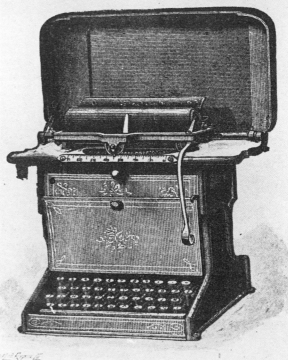

For flexible baleen filaments for watch-springs, umbrellas, toys
   and upholstery,
Even the springs in the first typewriter...

Millions and millions and millions died in a marine holocaust,
Generating the implacable human appetite for electricity,
   petroleum and plastic.

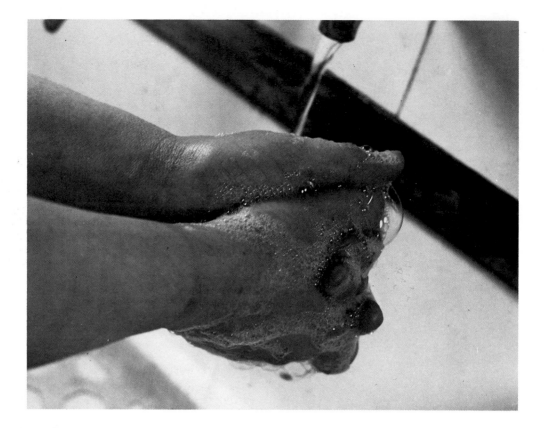

For soap, to be returned, mixed with dirt, into the sea;
For margarine;

For glycerol for lipstick, and the idle fantasy world of
   beauticians;
For detergents, from whose froth modern advertising was
   spawned;

For glycerine for nitro-glycerine, to blow a hole in the human herd;

For brushes and brooms;
For linoleum;
For medical trusses;

For oil-cloth;
For sausage skins;
For drum-skins;
For sword-hilts and scabbards;

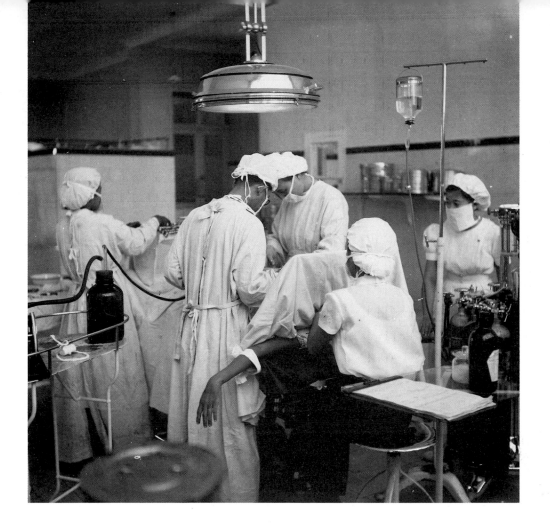

For laces;
For surgical stitches;
For tennis racket strings;

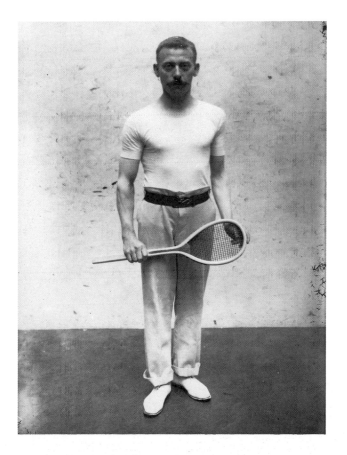

For riding crops;
For chess-men;
For buttons;
For tanning leather;
For artists' pigments;
For wax crayons;
For engineering coolants;
For golf-bags;

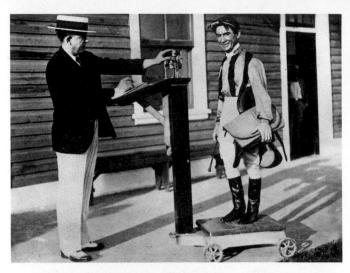

For varnishes;
For parchment;
For printing inks;
For insecticide;
For calcium for Blanco, and military purification;
For calcium for fertiliser, to speed up the gestation of the earth;

For the jute industry;
For the wool industry;
For the shoe industry;
For the cotton industry;
For tempering steel...

Without the blood-letting of the whale:
Prime source of light and lubrication,
The industrial revolution would have been scantily equipped.

A spectral colossus haunts the inflated myth of progress,
So keen to brush aside its hidden costs,
In the cause of pure profit;
So forgetful in the bright name of novelty.

For paint;
For skin cream;
For stock-cubes;
For cattle fencing;
For mah-jong counters;
For iodine;
For endocrinal hormones for those stiffened by arthritis;
For liver-oil and vitamins to treat those who are flagging;
For insulin from the pancreas to treat those whose blood is too
    sweet;
For gelatine for the coating of photographic film,
With which we see ourselves as we see ourselves, incessantly;
For gelatine for the transparent capsules of pills;
For gelatine for jelly;
For gelatine for glue;
For stays, and gussets, and busks, and bodices,
And statuesque corsetry, emphasising the breasts and hips:
The aesthetic apparatus, the sensual sustenance
Of empire building...

For fish-bait;
For cattle-meal;
For the food supplies to fur-farms;
For dog-food;
For cat-food;

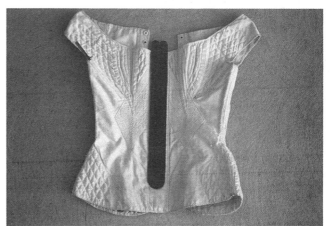

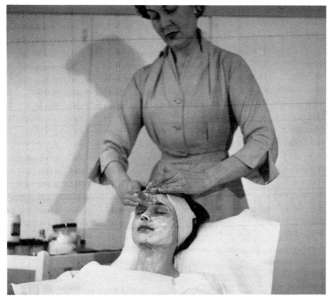

For the fermentation process in the manufacture of antibiotics;
For oiling the automatic transmission systems of automobiles;
For anti-freeze;
For low-calorie cooking fat;
For shortening for bread, and pastry, and cakes;
For hair treatments;
For bath essence;
For steaks: *sashimi* slices and marinated *yamotami*,
For *kujira nabe* and *obayuki* soup,
For whale-meat rissoles;
For whale-meat stew;
For pipes, for piano keys, for ear-rings, for brooches, for
   cuff-links;

For cigarette holders;
For shoe-horns;
For car-wax;
For shoe-polish;
For plasticiser;
For fishing-rods;
For machine oil . . .

For ambergris, burned in religious ceremonies
To put you in good odour with the Almighty;
For cosmetics, to put you in good odour with each other.

The sullen killing continues.
The killing of the largest creatures in the world.
It is unthinkingly supposed
That the rest of life will not be shrivelled in the process.

Large creatures disappear;
Life becomes smaller...

Blind dwarves
Crawl on top of the corpses of slaughtered giants
To see further into their impending solitude:
Gentle, visionary giants
Most fully appreciated when dead
And reassuringly unreal.

First, the Greenland whales...eliminated;
Then the Right whales,
So-called because they were judged to be the 'right' whales to
   kill;
Then the Humpbacks;
Then the Great Sperm whales, then the Blue;
Then Bryde's whales, then the Tasman;
Then the Gray whales, then the Fin;
Then the Piked whales, then the Sei;
Then the Minkes, then the Pilots...
All reduced to a precious few.

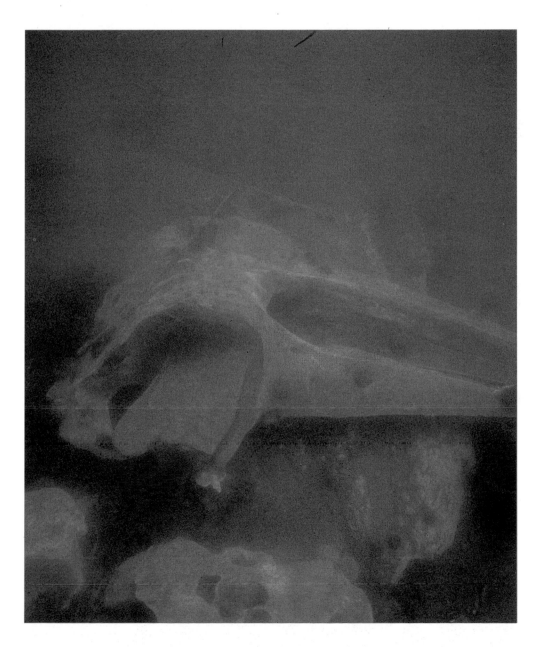

And now the dolphin:
The Spinners, the Blackchins, the Helmets;
The Snubfins, the Duskies, the Bottle-nosed;
The Bridled, the Spotted, the Melon-heads;
The Risso, the Peale's, the Heavisides;
The Hector's, the Whitebeaks, the Piebald;
The Irrawaddy, the Amazon, the Hourglass...
Two hundred and fifty thousand a year, netted and killed.

History relates that whales have only eaten one human: Jonah,
A prophet.
Ingested briefly, in the fond hope perhaps
Of learning something of the humans' Forward Planner,
And then disgorged.

The god Apollo saw the smallest whale, the dolphin,
As the embodiment of peaceful virtue, undisguised joy,
And as a guide to another world.
He sometimes exchanged his god-like status
To assume dolphin form;
And founded the oracle at Delphi,
Named in the dolphin's honour.
There, the god hoped,
Man might be guided by a sense of other-worldliness.

Two thousand five hundred years later,
Desacralised man
Strives to assimilate the dolphin in less mysterious ways,
By lifting its hydrodynamic shape to sophisticate the design of
     submarine weapons;
By confining it in small boxes, filled with stale water, as a
     scientific pet;

Or as a short-lived tourist attraction,
Bribed, with dead fish, to convey a repetitive sense of fun;
Or, by killing it, and tinning it, and eating it.

When dolphins speak
They use only vowels, and just faint hints of consonants,
But recognisable:

'Hello. How are you.
One-two-three-four-five . . . six-seven.
Yes. No.
A.E.I.O.U.
My name is Elvar. My name is Peter.
My name is Bobo. Clown.
It is six o'clock.
Trick. Squirt water. Trick. More water . . . Bye . . . bye bye.'

The bleak pleas of captives
Thinking that if this anxious imitation
Of their captors' speech finds favour,
Their experimental tanks may be changed for the open sea.

Tanks in which every sound they make underwater
Remorselessly bounces back at them from concrete walls,
Entwining their minds in an acoustic cat's-cradle.
Tanks in which they are blinded in the name of science.

But the more words they are coaxed into saying,
The cleverer they are thought to be.
The more successfully they communicate,
The longer they are required to stay.
'Look, they are just like us. Listen.'

And they find themselves flattered to death:
'Good boy, good boy.
Say good boy.'

'Good boy...'

In Ancient Greece it was thought
That nothing diviner than the dolphin
Had ever been created.
It was thought that they were once men,
Who had lived in cities, along with mortals;

That they had exchanged the land for the sea,
Taking the form of fishes;
But that they had retained the righteous spirit of man,
Retained human thought, and could perform human deeds.
Because of this, the killing of a dolphin
Carried the penalty of death...
A punishment which may yet be on the books.

Cetacean oil,
Cunningly used to protect the whale's sound-library from the
    cold,
Is extracted by hard-nosed, gimlet-eyed parasites
Who view the whale only as an industrial resource,
And eat through their musical society like deaf maggots –
Land-lubbing whale-lice,
Unable to detect the presence of oil
In the body of a fellow creature
Without desiring to suck it out.

Cetacean oil:
Oil that does not corrode,
Does not film over,
Does not go rancid,
Does not react to temperature changes;
Oil that can withstand the extreme cold of outer space,
Without losing its viscosity;
Irreplaceable sperm oil
Is stolen to provide the highest grade of lubricant...
Stock-piled, and prized beyond all others,
By the manufacturers of arms
To anoint the moving parts of missiles.

...Though this particular motor lubricant
May lead to all human cities clogged with rubble;

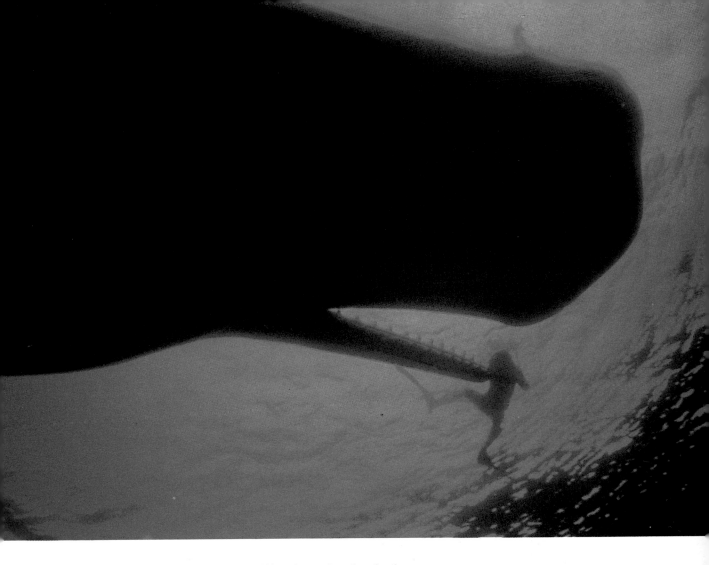

Ending their existence like beached whales,
Washed-up and rotting on the foreshores of civilisation,
Whose foundations were built upon dead blubber.

When Orion boasted
That he would kill all the animals in the world,
The earth sent a monstrous scorpion
To sting him.

In classical times, the rare stranding of a single whale,
Was taken as an omen of the death of a loved one.

In modern times, the mass stranding of whales,
Prompted by the disorienting noise of tankers, liners,
    depth-charges, warships,
And the corruption of the oceans with waste, with radiation,
Is taken to indicate the inferior intelligence of whales,
And ignored.

In accordance with some private harmony,
Whales appear out of the blue
To allow men to ride upon their backs;
To save them from sharks;
To rescue drowning men, even massaging their hearts.

Sometimes a dolphin,
With a mixture of saintliness and mischief,
Will try to bring round a body in the water
By employing the final act of intimacy.

When whaling boats have been overturned
And men have found themselves floundering helplessly in the
    seas,
They have been pushed up to the surface like bunches of frogs:
Forgivingly nudged by fellow mammals, until they regained
    their breath,
Tolerantly supported on a whale's back until they revived,
To kill again.

In the Koganji Temple in Yamaguchi Province
Tombs have been built to dead whales.
The monuments are facing the sea;
Thus, it is thought, the whales may pay homage to their dead.

The inscription upon one reads:
'You whales who have perished,
Although you cannot return to the world,
We will cherish your memory long in our hearts.'

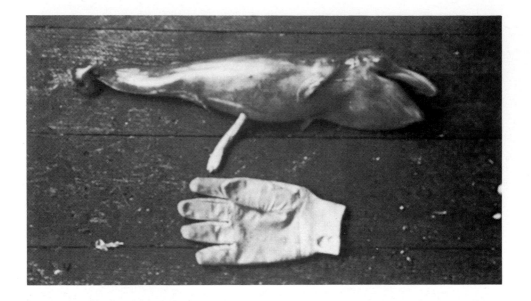

In Arikawara there is a memorial to six hundred whales;
In the Chudoji Temple of Muroto, there is a shrine for a
  thousand.
Beside the graves of embryo whales,
Each year, in Yamaguchi, a ceremony is conducted
In memory of the souls of the unborn,
And to lift a curse on man for killing so many whales.

In the water, whales have become the dominant species,
Without killing their own kind.

In the water, whales have become the dominant species,
Though they allow the resources they use to renew themselves.

In the water, whales have become the dominant species,
Though they use language to communicate, rather than to
eliminate rivals.

In the water, whales have become the dominant species,
Though they do not broodily guard their patch with bristling
security.

In the water, whales have become the dominant species,
Without trading innocence for the pretension of possessions.

In the water, whales have become the dominant species,
Though they acknowledge minds other than their own.

In the water, whales have become the dominant species,
Without allowing their population to reach plague proportions.

In the water, the whale is the dominant species;
An extra-terrestrial, who has already landed...

A marine intelligentsia, with a knowledge of the deep.

From space, the planet is blue.
From space, the planet is the territory
Not of humans, but of the whale.

On the Nature of Whales

We do not associate the idea of antiquity with the ocean, nor wonder how it looked a thousand years ago, as we do of the land, for it was equally wild and unfathomable always . . . The ocean is a wilderness reaching round the globe, wilder than a Bengal jungle . . .

Henry David Thoreau, *Cape Cod*, Boston: Ticknor and Fields, 1865

In A.D. 890, Ohthere, a Norwegian, made a voyage to the White Sea and on his return visited King Alfred of England to whom he related that he had seen whales 'eight and forty ells long'. Since an ell is 45 inches this makes the whales 180 feet long . . .

F. D. Ommanney, *Lost Leviathan*, London: Hutchinson, 1958

During the millions of years that life has existed on earth many exotic animals have appeared. People generally think that the largest of them must have been some dinosaur of the Mesozoic Age. One of them, *Brachiosaurus*, was a giant that weighed an estimated 50 tons. But such a giant was a runt compared to the blue whale, which weighs 50 tons long before the age of puberty. Indeed, a large female blue whale can lose 50 tons while nursing a calf and still weigh twice as much as *Brachiosaurus*. Most dinosaurs were so small that they could pass through the jawbone of a blue whale. Even in terms of length the blue whale remains superlative. *Diplodocus*, an herbivorous Jurassic dinosaur, reached an estimated length of almost 100 feet; blue whales have exceeded that by many feet. The blue whale, therefore, is the largest animal known to have lived on land or sea since the beginning of time.

George L. Small, *The Blue Whale*, New York: Columbia University Press, 1971

Cetaceans evolved brains the size of ours thirty million years ago. Our brains have only been their present size for approximately 100,000 years.

David Pilbeam, *Ascent of Man: Introduction to Human Evolution*, London: Thames and Hudson, 1972

We, as relative newcomers, may be asking too much of ourselves to communicate meaningfully with minds as ancient as those of the whales and dolphins . . . the whales and dolphins may have more to teach us than we have to teach them.

John C. Lilly, *Man and Dolphin*, New York: Doubleday, 1961

The whales, properly, take up most of our attention as the mammals most completely adapted to an aquatic habitat and with the longest history of that adaptation. The history of the brain in whales is a history of early enlargement, dating to the zeuglodonts (suborder Archaeoceti) of the Eocene, and dramatically notable by the Miocene in the ancestors of living porpoises.

It seems likely that whales, including small species such as porpoises and dolphins, achieved their modern enlarged brains in Miocene times, about 15–20 million years ago . . . the evolution of the whales was associated with the evolution of sensory and sensorimotor adaptations for manœuvring in water, and, even more dramatically, the evolution of the auditory and sound producing systems for echolocation and for the perception of objects by their echoes. The enlargement of the acoustic component, the inferior colliculi of the midbrain, the entire cerebral cortex, and, in association with the cortex, the cerebellum were all parts of these adaptations.

The comparative anatomy of the brain of the whale is becoming a more popular topic among neuroanatomists, and one can expect more information on specific adaptations shown by the whales. The enormous expansion of the neocortex in living whales is the most interesting of the adaptations, since relative to the brain as a whole the bottlenose dolphin, for one, exceeds even man in this regard. The evidence from paleoneurology adds a dimension of time to findings such as these because, as far as one can judge from endocasts and estimates of body size, this may have been an ancient adaptation that has characterized the cetaceans during the past 15 or 20 million years at least. The evolution of the human brain is a phenomenon of the past few million years at most . . .

Harry J. Jerison, *Evolution of the Brain and Intelligence*, New York: Academic Press, 1973

Cetaceans unquestionably have big brains and the frequency with which they use them in patterns that can only be described as play suggests that they frolic with their minds as readily as they do with their bodies. This tendency towards mental playfulness may in itself have been partly responsible for the enlargement of their brains.

Lyall Watson and Tom Ritchie, *Whales of the World*, London: Hutchinson, 1981

Two dolphins enjoyed playing with an eel in their tank. One of the dolphins would catch the eel delicately between its teeth, carry it around for a while, then let it go. The other dolphin would then catch the eel and swim around with it, chased by her friend. They would then reverse the chase. One day the eel managed to hide in a pipe at the bottom of the tank. The dolphin found a small poisonous fish that also lived in the tank. He carefully caught the fish in his teeth so that it couldn't hurt him, and poked the fish into the pipe where the eel was hiding. The eel zoomed out and the dolphins continued their game of catch.

Karl-Erik Fichtelius and Sverre Sjölander, *Man's Place: Intelligence in Whales, Dolphins, and Humans*, London: Gollancz, 1973

The dolphin is an animal not only friendly to man, but a lover of music as well. He is charmed by melodious concerts, especially by the notes of the water organ. He does not dread man, as though a stranger to him, but comes to meet ships, leaps and bounds to and fro, vies with them in swiftness, and passes them even in full sail.

Pliny the Elder (A.D. 23–79), *Naturalis Historia*, ed. Mayhoff, Leipzig, 1909

For the space of a few minutes, they are capable of darting through the water, with the velocity of the fastest ship under sail, and of ascending with such rapidity as to leap entirely out of the water.

W. Scoresby Jnr F.R.S.E., *An Account of the Arctic Regions, with a History and Description of the Northern Whale-Fishery*, Edinburgh: Archibald Constable, 1820

When swimming fast, many cetaceans jump clear out of the water while breathing. There are sound hydrodynamic reasons for this. If a whale exposes part of its body in bringing the blowhole to the surface, it meets maximum turbulence and drag. By jumping clear out of the water it can maintain speed without expending too much energy.

Lyall Watson and Tom Ritchie, *Whales of the World*, London: Hutchinson, 1981

Bulky as the whale is, and inactive, or indeed clumsy as it appears to be, one might imagine that all its motions would be sluggish, and its greatest exertions productive of no great celerity. The fact, however, is the reverse. A whale extended motionless at the surface of the sea, can sink in the space of five or six seconds, or less, beyond the reach of its human enemies.

W. Scoresby Jnr F.R.S.E., *An Account of the Arctic Regions, with a History and Description of the Northern Whale-Fishery*, Edinburgh: Archibald Constable, 1820

All sperm whales both large and small, have some method of communicating by signals to each other, by which they become apprised of the approach of danger, and this they do, although the distance may be very considerable between them, sometimes amounting to four, five or even seven miles. The mode by which this is effected, remains a curious secret.

Thomas Beale, *The Natural History of the Sperm Whale, to Which is Added a Sketch of a South-Sea Whaling Voyage*, London: John van Voorst, 1839

The third day . . . we sighted whales again. We lowered three boats as promptly as usual; but when within about half a mile of the 'pod' some slight noise in one of the boats galled them, and away they went in the wind's eye, it blowing a stiffish breeze at the time. It was from the first evidently a hopeless task to chase them, but we persevered until recalled to the ship, dead beat with fatigue . . . In passing, I would like to refer to the wonderful way in which these whales realize at a great distance, if the slightest sound be made, the presence of danger. I do not use the word 'hear' because so abnormally small are their organs of hearing, the external opening being quite difficult to find, that I do not believe they *can* hear at all well. But I firmly believe they possess another sense by means of which they are able to detect any unusual vibration of the waves of either air or sea at a far greater distance than it would be possible for them to hear. Whatever this power may be which they possess, all whalemen are well acquainted with their exercise of it, and always take the most elaborate precautions to render their approach to a whale noiseless.

Frank T. Bullen, *The Cruise of the 'Cachalot' Round the World after Sperm Whales*, Beccles (Suffolk): Smith Elder, 1898

By 1951 SOFAR (sound fixing and ranging) stations had been set up around the world and were beginning to add to the whalers' knowledge. Many of the oddest sounds seem to have been produced by cetaceans. A widespread low-frequency 'moan' at about 20 Hz in the background almost anywhere in temperate waters has now been identified [W. E. Schevill 'Underwater Sounds of Cetaceans', in *Marine Bioacoustics*, ed. W. M. Tavolga, Oxford: Pergamon, 1964] as the voice of the Fin Whale, perhaps with occasional choruses by the vanishing Blue Whale. Low-frequency 'thumps' between 100 and 200 Hz, which crop up so often in hydrophone records that they have come to be known to analysts as the 'A train', were identified only in 1976 as emanating from the Piked Whale [H. E. Winn and P. J. Perkins, 'Distribution and Sounds of the Minke Whale', in *Cetology*, 19, pp. 1–12, 1976]. A strange 'boing' about four seconds long at a frequency of 100 Hz has been recorded in the Pacific and still remains to be identified [G. M. Wenz, 'Curious Noises and the Sonic Environment in the Sea', in *Marine Bioacoustics*, ed. W. M. Tavolga, Oxford: Pergamon, 1964].

The 'thump trains' of Piked Whales, the moans of Fin Whales and the whistles of Humpback Whales all have distinctive frequencies and repetition rates which make it possible for human listeners, and therefore presumably whales, to recognize individual animals over great distances.

A Blue Whale's whistle recorded at 188 decibels is the loudest sound ever known to be produced by any living source and, with power exceeding that even of a passing jet plane (usually between 140 and 170 decibels), will certainly travel considerable distances underwater [W. C. Cummings and P. O. Thompson, 'Underwater Sounds from the Blue Whale', *Journal of the Acoustical Society of America*, 50, pp. 1193–8, 1971].

Lyall Watson and Tom Ritchie, *Whales of the World*, London: Hutchinson, 1981

You have probably never heard anything like this, because it is so low, approximately 20 hertz, or just at the threshold of our hearing. Many people compare listening to the blue whales to the experience of sensing an earthquake. The vibrations count as much as the sound.

Ronn Storro-Patterson, cited in Ted Crail, *Apetalk & Whalespeak: The Quest for Interspecies Communication*, Los Angeles/Boston: J. P. Tarcher/Houghton Mifflin, 1981

The song [of the humpback whale] is repeated . . . and emitted with sound intensities of 100 to 110 decibels, that is to say, in a class with a pneumatic drill. What is most interesting in this context is that the song was heard at a depth of about 3,300 feet off the east coast of North America, which is just at the depth where we find two sound-reflecting layers close to each other. (These layers exist in all the oceans, at various depths.) Our calculations indicate that a sound of this intensity, emitted within the reflecting layers, could be heard by a human ear at a distance of well over 25,000 miles (which is the circumference of the earth). Even if we make deductions for disturbance, background noise, and the like, it appears that by seeking out this communication layer whales could call to each other over distances as great as the entire breadth of the Pacific Ocean. If the humpback whale can use this system, then there is every reason to believe that the sperm whale can use it as well.

Karl-Erik Fichtelius and Sverre Sjölander, *Man's Place, Intelligence in Whales, Dolphins, and Humans*, London: Gollancz, 1973

Water is a much better conductor of sound than air. Although the values are affected by the water temperature, sound travels approximately five times faster in water than it does in air. If there are no obstructions or interfering sounds (such as the noise of boat engines), low frequency sound can travel for hundreds of miles under water. The sound of depth charges off Australia was heard off Bermuda, half way round the world.

At a depth roughly calculated to be between 600 and 1200 metres, there is a thermocline known as the deep sound channel, which retains a proportion of underwater sound, and enables it to travel for enormous distances. If the humpbacks are able to utilize this channel, it may be that they are able to communicate with any other humpback, in any ocean where they are not separated by land.

Richard Ellis, 'New Light on the Whale Song Mystery', *San Francisco Chronicle*, June 1978

The host of unlike voices transform the sea into a party line from which each subscriber picks out his own messages. If François Rabelais could live again and hear them, he might wonder why four centuries elapsed without men of science giving attention to these sounds. His hero, Pantagruel, discoursed on the subject with the Skipper, and was told that the noises he heard at night from the sea were sounds from a battle the preceding winter, frozen solid in the air at that time and just now thawing out to become audible again. Calls from the abyss do come from water close to the freezing point.

Lorus J. Milne and Margery Milne, *The Senses of Animals and Men*, London: André Deutsch, 1963

A whale would sometimes get under the boat . . . and there utter the most doleful sounds, interspersed with a gurgling sound such as a drowning man might make. The first time I heard these sounds it was almost incomprehensible to me that they could proceed from a whale.

Charles Nordhoff, *Whaling and Fishing*, Cincinnati: Moore, Wilstach, and Keys, 1856

In 1967 Roger Payne of the Rockefeller University turned from a study of the ability of owls to hear and locate their prey in total darkness to the equally mysterious underwater vocalizations of Humpback Whales. Every spring until 1971 he and his wife Katherine floated in the waters of the whales' breeding ground near Bermuda, recording their long, repeating patterns of sound. These 'song cycles' are now believed to be the most elaborate single display known in any animal species.

Lyall Watson and Tom Ritchie, *Whales of the World*, London: Hutchinson, 1981

Large scale progressive changes were observed in humpback songs from Bermuda in a sample containing 13 of the 18 years between 1957 and 1975 . . . At any given moment, all singing whales sang the same version of their song, but after a year or more, that version had disappeared and was replaced by a new version. As time went on, the song became increasingly different from the earliest version recorded. The extent of the changes from one year to the next varied, but in times of rapid change it only took a few years for every part of the song to be altered beyond recognition.

New variations in the song must be transmitted by learning. The progressive changes in whale song can thus be seen as a form of cultural evolution, in the sense that the song is a learned trait which evolves.

Our recordings provide evidence that the changes in song are not simply due to forgetfulness between singing seasons. Most changes did not occur between seasons. Instead, they occurred during the time when the whales were singing, developing their songs methodically in measurable steps. Furthermore, the types of change varied from season to season, and so could not be attributed to repeating seasonal factors.

We know of no other animal where whole populations introduce such complex, rapid and non-reversing changes into their vocal displays, abandoning old forms and replacing them with new. It is not clear what selective advantage would be obtained by changing songs continuously . . .

Songs are composed of a series of discrete notes, or units. We define units as the shortest sounds in the song which seem continuous to the human ear. Small repeated groups of units are called phrases. Phrases are usually uniform in duration. Many phrases consist of two subphrases, which may in themselves contain repeated sounds. All phrases of one kind make up a theme. Themes may contain any number of phrases and so their length is extremely variable.

We say a whale is singing when we hear groups of units repeated. A song is a series of different themes given in a predictable order. Successive songs are sung without pauses between them, and we refer to all songs in an unbroken sequence as a song session. The longest continuous excerpt from a song session which we recorded lasted 10·5 hours; however, the complete session was longer, as the whale was already singing when we found it and still singing when we were forced to leave it . . .

Not only is there a turnover of units or alternate phrases within each of them, but entire themes gradually die out and new ones appear. Two themes were sung less and less frequently; both were finally omitted from the song. We have also witnessed the birth of new themes. In 1979 a completely novel sound entered the song, became a pattern of phrases and established its own place in the orderly progression of themes. Whether this sound was spontaneously invented and then imitated, whether it was developed from material in the songs that we did not happen to record, or whether it reflects interchange with whales that had learned phrases from another dialect, we do not know.

Katherine Payne, Peter Tyack and Roger Payne, 'Progressive Changes in the Songs of Humpback Whales (*Megaptera novaeangliae*): A Detailed Analysis of Two Seasons in Hawaii', in *Communication and Behaviour in Whales*, Washington DC: American Association for the Advancement of Science, Selected Symposium, 1983

Humpback whales sing songs that change over time. They also sing different songs in different areas. In the eastern North Pacific, two widely separated wintering grounds for humpbacks are occupied by individuals singing the same song. We have analysed over 70 humpback songs from Hawaii and the Revillagigedo Islands recorded in 1977 and 1979. Although these wintering grounds are 4700 km apart, the song in both places has remained the same throughout this period – changes in one area paralleling changes in the other. This surprising result strongly suggests that the animals in these widely separated places are part of the same population.

Since songs change continuously and individual singers adopt new material sung by the other singers in an area, we can conclude that two whales singing the same song either are in direct acoustic contact or are linked by a chain of acoustic contact involving other whales.

Roger Payne and Linda N. Guinee, 'Humpback Whale (*Megaptera novaeangliae*): Songs as an Indicator of "Stocks"', in *Communication and Behaviour in Whales*, Washington DC: American Association for the Advancement of Science, Selected Symposium, 1983

On three occasions I approached adults who were singing songs so loud they appeared to come through one's whole body . . .

Deborah A. Glockner, 'Determining the Sex of Humpback Whales (*Megaptera novaeangliae*) in Their Natural Environment', from *Communication and Behaviour in Whales*, Washington DC: American Association for the Advancement of Science, Selected Symposium, 1983

No word conveys the eeriness of the whale song, tuned by the ages to a purity beyond refining, a sound that man should hear each morning to remind him of the morning of the world.

Peter Matthiessen, *Blue Meridian*, New York: Random House, 1971

The hump appeared, she blew and sounded and, a few seconds later, was passing directly under the dory. It seemed to take as long for the interminable sweep of her body to slip by as it does for a train to pass a railway crossing. But so smoothly and gently did she pass that we felt no motion except when the vast flukes went under us and the dory bobbed a little.

It was then I heard the voice of the Fin Whale . . . It was a long, low sonorous moan with unearthly overtones in a higher pitch. It was unbelievably weird and bore no affinity with any sound I have heard from any other living thing. It was a voice not of the world we know.

Farley Mowat, *A Whale for the Killing*, London: Heinemann, 1973

Payne has recorded examples of very long songs sung by the humpback whale; some of the songs were as long as half an hour or more. A few of them appear to be repeatable, virtually phoneme by phoneme; somewhat later the entire cycle of sounds comes out virtually identically once again. Some of the songs have been commercially recorded and are available on CRM Records (SWR-II). I calculate that the approximate number of bits of information (individual yes/no questions necessary to characterize the song) in a whale song of half an hour's length is between a million and a hundred million bits. Because of the very large frequency variation in these songs, I have assumed that the frequency is important in the context of the song – or, put another way, that whale language is tonal. If it is not as tonal as I guess, the number of bits in such a song may go down by a factor of ten . . .

Carl Sagan, *The Cosmic Connection*, New York: Doubleday, 1973

Voyager I and Voyager II, in their billion-year space journey, are carrying whale sounds as well as human sounds. Should contact be made with inhabitants of other civilizations, other universes, they will have these samples of earth sound to judge us by.

Ted Crail, *Apetalk & Whalespeak: The Quest for Interspecies Communication*, Los Angeles/Boston: J. P. Tarcher/Houghton Mifflin, 1981

No apparent relationship exists between migratory paths and oceanic currents and water masses. Humpbacks may travel with or against surface currents, and over every sort of bottom topography. This may indicate that humpbacks use navigational aids such as the sun, the moon, stars, magnetic fields, or sound to find their way in the oceans. The study of the movements of humpbacks is really just beginning.

Lois King Winn and Howard E. Winn, *Wings in the Sea: The Humpback Whale*, New Hampshire: University Press of New England, 1985

Visibility under water is much poorer than it is on land, since a great deal of light is absorbed by the upper layers of water. Thus, off our coasts, 90 per cent of white light is absorbed by the time we go down to five fathoms, and only 1 per cent of white light penetrates below twenty fathoms. Below 215 fathoms, the sea is pitch black, no matter how clear the water or how bright the sunshine. Horizontal visibility is further decreased by the scarcity of light-reflecting objects . . . In other words, big whales would be unable to see their own flukes. Since, moreover, many Cetaceans spend part of their time below the ice where only a very small amount of light penetrates, and since many of them are predominantly nocturnal animals, it is not surprising that vision does not play as important a part for them as for other mammals.

E. J. Slijper, *Whales*, London: Hutchinson, 1962

Sound behaves somewhat differently from light. For one thing, it penetrates much better, bending round corners and passing through things . . . The dolphin emits a steady stream of sounds called clicks . . . each one lasting only 10 to 100 milliseconds . . . When an echo signalling a fish is received, the dolphin turns and swims towards its source. As the animal approaches its prey, it clicks faster and faster, often seven hundred times a second. Judging distance by the interval between the emitted clicks and returning echoes, and determining the fish's speed and course by picking up shifts in the echo frequencies, the dolphin closes in and snatches up its prey with the accuracy of a hawk plucking a mouse from a meadow.

The fat surrounding the jaws carries sound waves in, where they vibrate the bulla and the ossicles and set the cochlear fluid in motion. When a dolphin inspects some new object by echolocation, it rotates its head about the target as it listens. Various frequencies have different abilities to penetrate the jawbone . . . By rotating its head and thus changing the angle of the jaws to the source of the echoes, the dolphin can determine the frequencies of the sounds and identify what it has under sonic scrutiny . . .

In the depths two or three thousand feet below the surface, sperm whales chase and catch giant squid in total darkness. Pelagic porpoises hunt fish on moonless nights so completely black that one questions the inevitability of sunrise. And bottlenose dolphins swim up narrow channels thick with mud, thread mazes of shoals and bars, catch fish fleeing at full speed, then find their way back to the sea; all without colliding with each other, the bank, or some underwater obstacle . . .

Some cetaceans produce sounds with, and are presumably equipped to detect echoes from, frequencies higher than 200 kHz, with which they can distinguish objects as small as vertical wires 0·35 mm (less than ·015 inch) in diameter.

Robert McNally, 'Echolocation, Cetaceans' Sixth Sense', *Oceans*, 55 (vol. 10, no. 4), San Francisco, July–August 1977

One clear advantage the dolphin has over us is that it can, in all probability, listen *through* objects. Sound waves in water penetrate a dolphin or a human being with only the loss of a little reflection and absorption. Skin, muscle, and fat are virtually transparent to sound waves carried by water. Air cavities and bone, on the other hand, reflect sound waves relatively strongly – the air cavities in particular. A dolphin 'listening' to another dolphin hears the body contours diffusely, teeth and bone somewhat better, and those parts containing air – the alimentary canal, the breathing passages including the lungs, and the air cavities in the skull – quite distinctly. The dolphin hears in a way that resembles the way a roentgenologist uses X-rays to see. This must have considerable emotional significance for the communication of emotional states and thus for all personal interaction . . . Dolphins probably have a hard time dissembling. We express a part of our feelings with our facial muscles, which can be consciously controlled. Dolphins reveal themselves, among other ways, through intestinal peristalsis, which is not directly under the influence of the will. It is impossible for one dolphin to play tough with another. People who have difficulty communicating their feelings will easily appreciate the advantage that dolphins enjoy in this respect.

Karl-Erik Fichtelius and Sverre Sjölander, *Man's Place: Intelligence in Whales, Dolphins and Humans*, London: Gollancz, 1973

The result is a system [of hearing] so sensitive that a dolphin in a large tank can hear a teaspoonful of water being poured into it anywhere and still turn and fix that spot precisely.

Lyall Watson and Tom Ritchie, *Whales of the World*, London: Hutchinson, 1971

Trainers working with captive animals report that these have no difficulty in distinguishing the sex of humans in the water, react differently to each one and seem even to be aware of menstrual cycles.

Lyall Watson and Tom Ritchie, *Whales of the World*, London: Hutchinson, 1981

At Kaneohe near Oahu, Hawaii, the testing ground for porpoises operated by the Naval Ocean Systems Centre, a female dolphin would choose between red and blue 'paddles' in response to a series of questions put to her by Earl Murchison. Red was for yes, blue was for no. The questions were always about objects dropped in the ocean.

'Is there anything out there?'

The trainer speaks his question in English so that humans will understand it, but it is represented to the dolphin as an electronic tone. If the drop has been faked and nothing has been put in the ocean, the female dolphin reports this faithfully by choosing the blue (no) paddle. When an object is actually dropped, the question 'Is anything out there?' is followed by another: 'Is it a cylinder?'

'Yes.'

'Is it stationary?'

'Yes.' (They have it suspended.)

'Is the next one stationary?'

'No.' (They have let it go.)

Whether the object is aluminium or wood, brass or steel, long or short, big or small, she touches the correct colour to answer the questions. When she says no, she sometimes 'snorts a bubble from her blowhole' as though to give the rejection emphasis.

She can perform the cylinder-identification test just as reliably when the cylinders are dropped, in murky water, well beyond her visual range. She is now identifying the objects through her acoustical system alone. Sight does not play a part.

Ted Crail, *Apetalk & Whalespeak: The Quest for Interspecies Communication*, Los Angeles/Boston: J. P. Tarcher/Houghton Mifflin, 1981

Since the dolphin employs frequencies $4\frac{1}{2}$ times higher than the ones we use, its sound-producing apparatus can manage $4\frac{1}{2}$ times as much information per unit of time. The dolphin appears to have two separate sets of sound-producing apparatus, one in each half of its blowhole. They can be used simultaneously. This means that the dolphin ought to be able to emit 9 times as much information as we can per unit of time.

Now the fact is that when used together, these two sets of sound apparatus produce a stereophonic effect, which ought logically to increase their informational capacity in relation to ours beyond a factor of 9. If we say that the dolphin can emit 10 times as much physical information via sound as we can, then that is probably an underestimate.

Karl-Erik Fichtelius and Sverre Sjölander, *Man's Place: Intelligence in Whales, Dolphins and Humans*, London: Gollancz, 1973

After training a blindfold female Bottlenose Dolphin to recognize a copper plate by its acoustic properties, William Evans of the Naval Undersea Center in San Diego presented her with glass, plastic and aluminium imitations of the same size and shape. She immediately dismissed these as counterfeits. He then tested her with an aluminium plate whose thickness had been calculated to have exactly the same sonic reflectivity as copper, but she still picked out the copper correctly. To do this she had not only to perceive the basic feature of the echoes but also their precise frequency composition. What makes this performance even more impressive is that, to do it all, she had to remember the frequency mix in the copper echo, analyse the sound from the aluminium copy, and then compare the two for subtle proportional differences. She completed this sophisticated exercise in a matter of seconds.

Lyall Watson and Tom Ritchie, *Whales of the World*, London: Hutchinson, 1981

The question has been raised whether dolphins communicate with each other with the help of something that might be compared to human speech. The following experiment . . . was carried out by Dr. Jarvis Bastian in the United States.

A male and a female were presented with two keys and a single light. When the light was steady they were to depress the key on the right; when it was blinking, the key on the left. If they did it correctly – and they quickly learned to do so – they were rewarded with a fish. Then a screen was placed between the animals so that only the female saw the signal light. When the first signal was given, the female swam up to her keys and uttered some dolphin sounds. The male then pressed the correct key of his pair, whereupon the female pressed the correct key on her side. The dolphins could repeat this trick as often as they 'wanted' to. Dr. Bastian, who performed the experiment, is himself very cautious in interpreting the results.

Karl-Erik Fichtelius and Sverre Sjölander, *Man's Place: Intelligence in Whales, Dolphins, and Humans*, London: Gollancz, 1973

It has long been suspected that porpoises, whales, and dolphins talk to one another, and these suspicions are now confirmed by scientific research. Their language is now in the process of being decoded.

Dr. John Dreher, a scientist of the Lockheed Aircraft Corporation, has gathered the evidence by recording the whistles of these large-brained, small-scale whales, while they played, exercised, and ate.

He analysed the whistles and found eighteen separate and distinct sound combinations. Of the eighteen 'sound contours', twelve could be assigned ranks as to frequencies of use. Sound contours ('phonemes') are the bricks of the edifice of language, ours or any other. The innumerable words of our language are combined with only twenty-six letters.

Dr. Dreher suggests that the whistle contours of the porpoise perhaps stand for syllables. Even with only eighteen contours or phonemes, a lot of significant messages or 'morphemes' could be combined.

Dr. Dreher is now trying to fit the tone contours of these animal whistles to their behaviour. Thus he may find out what the whistles mean: singly and in combination.

Elisabeth Mann Borgese, *The Language Barrier: Beasts and Men*, New York: Holt, Rinehart and Winston, 1968

For a voice the dolphin has a moaning or a wailing similar to that of the human.

Pliny the Elder (A.D. 23–79), *Naturalis Historia*, ed. Mayhoff, Leipzig, 1909

The voice of the dolphin in air is like that of the human in that they can pronounce vowels and combinations of vowels, but have difficulties with the consonants.

Aristotle (384–322 B.C.), *Historia Animalium*, trans. D'Arcy W. Thomson: Oxford University Press, 1910

The intricate combination of phenomena necessary for a complex language like ours could very well exist in other animals, for example, dolphins . . . But it may employ a logic that is entirely foreign to us, and treat information in a way that seems to us backwards.

The inborn biological, morphological, and physiological prerequisites for human language are a well-developed brain, something to talk about, and something to talk with. A comparison between dolphin and man in accordance with this list shows that on every point where we have adequate information, dolphins are superior to human beings.

Karl-Erik Fichtelius and Sverre Sjölander, *Man's Place: Intelligence in Whales, Dolphins, and Humans*, London: Gollancz, 1973

The defect that hinders communication betwixt them and us, why may it not be on our part as well as theirs? 'Tis yet to determine where the fault lies that we understand not one another; for we understand them no more than they do us; by the same reason they may think us to be beasts as we think them.

Michel de Montaigne, *Essays*, trans. Charles Cotton, London: T. Basset, 1693

On Mornington Island, in the Gulf of Carpentaria in Northern Australia, lives a tribe of Aborigines known as the Dolphin People. This tribe has been reported to be in direct communication with the wild bottlenose dolphins who reside just off the coast, and for many thousands of years as well. Their Shamans remain heir to a complex series of whistles that signal the dolphins to venture close to shore. Then the whistling first becomes more animated, and then stops altogether. The Shamans explain that, at that point, they begin to speak to the dolphins mind to mind.

Jim Nollman, *Dolphin Dreamtime: Talking to the Animals*, London: Anthony Blond, 1985

It was common enough in the Gilbert Islands that certain local clans had the power of porpoise-calling, but it was rather like the Indian rope trick; you never met anyone who had actually witnessed the thing . . .

Kitiona's own kinsmen in Kuma village, seventeen miles up-lagoon, were the hereditary porpoise-callers of the High Chiefs of Butaritari and Makin-Meang. His first cousin was a leading expert at the game; he could put himself into the right kind of dream on demand. His spirit went out of his body in such a dream; it sought out the porpoise-folk in their home under the western horizon and invited them to a dance, with feasting, in Kuma village. If he spoke the words of the invitation aright (and very few had the secret of them) the porpoise would follow him with cries of joy to the surface.

Having led them to the lagoon entrance, he would fly forward to rejoin his body and warn the people of their coming. It was quite easy for one who knew the way of it. The porpoise never failed to arrive. Would I like some called for me? After some rather idle shilly-shallying I admitted that I would; but did he think I should be allowed to see them coming? Yes, he replied, that could probably be arranged. He would talk to his kinsmen about it . . .

When the fat, friendly man who styled himself the High Chief's hereditary porpoise-caller came waddling down the beach to greet me, I asked when the porpoise would arrive. He said he would have to go into his dream first, but thought he could have them there for me by three or four o'clock.

Please though, he added firmly, would I be careful to call them, from now on, *only* 'our friends from the west'. The other name was tabu . . .

The hours dragged by and nothing happened. Four o'clock passed. My faith was beginning to sag under the strain when a strangled howl burst from the dreamer's hut. I jumped round to see his cumbrous body come hurtling head first through the torn screens. He sprawled on his face, struggled up, and staggered into the open, a slobber of saliva on his chin. He stood awhile clawing at the air and whining on a queer note like a puppy's. Then words came gulping out of him: 'Teirake! Teirake! (Arise! Arise!) . . . They come! . . . Our friends from the west . . . They come! Let us go down and greet them.' He started at a lumbering gallop down the beach . . . a man near me yelped and stood pointing; others took up his cry, but I could make out nothing for myself at first in the splintering glare of the sun. When at last I did see them . . . they were pretty near . . . gambolling towards us at a fine clip. When they came to the edge of the blue water by the reef,

they slackened speed, spread themselves out and started cruising back and forth in front of our line. Then, suddenly, there was no more of them.

In the strained silence that followed, I thought they were gone. The disappointment was so sharp I did not stop to think that, even so, I had seen a very strange thing. I was in the act of touching the dreamer's shoulder to take my leave when he turned his still face to me: 'The king out of the west comes to meet me,' he murmured, pointing . . . My eyes followed his hand. There, not ten yards away, was the great shape of a porpoise poised like a glimmering shadow in the glass-green water. Behind it followed a whole dusky flotilla of them. So slowly they came, they seemed to be hung in a trance.

Sir Arthur Grimble, *A Pattern of Islands*, London: John Murray, 1952

It seems that even dolphins are more scrupulous than men in showing their gratitude . . . One Coeranus by name, a native of Paros, when some dolphins fell into the net and were captured at Byzantium, gave their captors money, as it were a ransom, and set them at liberty; and for this he earned their gratitude. At any rate he was sailing once (so the story goes) in a fifty-oar ship with a crew of Milesians when the ship capsized in the strait between Naxos and Paros, and though all the rest were drowned, Coeranus was rescued by dolphins, which repaid the good deed that he had first done them by a similar deed. And the headland and caverned rock to which they swam with him on their backs are pointed out, and the spot is called Coeraneus. Later, when this same Coeranus died, they burned his body by the seashore. Whereupon the dolphins, observing this from some point, assembled as though they were attending his funeral, and all the while that the pyre was ablaze they remained at hand, as one trusty friend might remain by another. When at length the fire was quenched they swam away.

Men, however, are subservient to the wealthy and the seemingly prosperous while they are alive, but when dead or in misfortune they turn their backs upon them so as to avoid repaying them for past favours.

Aelian (fl. A.D. 210), *On the Characteristics of Animals*, vol. II, trans. A. F. Scholfield, London/Cambridge, Mass.: Heinemann/Harvard University Press, 1959

There is no doubt that we can communicate with the dolphin in many ways, either with signs or spoken language. There is no doubt that he in turn communicates with us on the response level, and to a limited degree (and here the shame is ours) perhaps even in English. The only gracious thing that man, as the king of the beasts, can do is to attempt to talk to the dolphin in his own code.

John J. Dreher, of Lockheed Aircraft, at the First International Symposium on Cetacean Research, sponsored by the American Institute of Biological Sciences, in Washington, DC, August 1963

After several weeks in captivity dolphins apparently learn that humans do not hear these sounds emitted under water very easily, and they begin to express their state by emitting such sounds in air above water aimed at the particular human involved.

When animals are first placed in captivity they tend to emit their sounds under water. Slowly but surely they begin to emit their sounds in air, keeping the delphinic patterns of sounds.

After several weeks of such noises one begins to notice a changing pattern of the airborne sounds to more complex sounds involving longer emissions, greater richness of selection of frequencies and harmonics. In our experience such changes occur if and only if people have been talking to the animals directly and very loudly individually. Slowly but surely these sounds become more and more like those of human speech.

The first copies of the human voice by the dolphin (in 1957 and 1958) were at a relatively low amplitude. The most recent ones on the part of our three current animals are sometimes painfully loud for the human observer.

The development of these sounds by a given dolphin . . . illustrate that the very large brain of Tursiops truncatus (20 to 40 per cent larger than that of the average human) may have within its complex structure speech capabilities, if not realized, at least potentially similar to those of humans.

John C. Lilly, 'Vocal Behaviour of the Bottlenose Dolphin', *Proceedings of the American Philosophical Society*, vol. 106, 1962

L illy also tells a scarcely believable story. On April 16, 1960, one of the dolphins, named Lizzie, seemed to be very ill: Lilly and his crew were trying to take care of her when over the loudspeaker, came the voice of someone calling the researchers to tell them they would miss dinner if they did not come right away.

'It's six o'clock,' it said.

Lilly answered the call and never again saw Lizzie, who died during the night.

Later, listening to the tape recorded in the aquarium that day, Lilly heard that urgent 'It's six o'clock,' and almost immediately afterward a series of whistles and a sentence in an almost human voice. The sentence could have been a bad imitation of 'It's six o'clock,' but Lilly and the rest of the people listening to the tape thought it sounded more like, 'This is a trick,' very clearly said, even if in no more of a hiss than a statement.

Was it a coincidence? An illusion?

Jacques Graven, *Non-Human Thought*, London: Arlington Books, 1968

T he feelings of weirdness came on us as the sounds of this small whale seemed more and more to be forming words in our own language. We felt we were in the presence of Something, or Someone who was on the other side of a transparent barrier which up to this point we hadn't even seen. The dim outlines of a Someone began to appear. We began to look at this whale's body with newly opened eyes and began to think in terms of its possible 'mental processes', rather than in terms of the classical view of a conditionable, instinctually functioning 'animal'.

John Lilly, 'Productive and Creative Research with Man and Dolphin', *Archives of General Psychiatry*, vol. VIII, Chicago: American Medical Association, 1963

A film exists, made by the Navy, which shows whales dressed in space-age headgear nosing down into the ocean, finding a lost torpedo, clamping a lifting device onto the torpedo with their special headgear, swimming confidently away as a parachute blooms from the device they have installed. The parachute lifts the torpedo to the surface . . .

In San Diego, I had spoken with Navy men familiar with the making of the film, and they had told me that not only were the whales marvellous at understanding the process the humans had taught them, but the whales soon felt they understood what was wanted better than clumsy sailors did. When the sailors fouled up, the whales would get sore and fuss – in gestures the humans could understand.

Ted Crail, *Apetalk & Whalespeak: The Quest for Interspecies Communication*, Los Angeles/Boston: J. P. Tarcher/Houghton Mifflin, 1981

How sharper than a sermon's truth it must have been for many human beings when they learned that bottle-nosed Dolphin may, in time, succeed battle-poised Man as the master species on earth. This prophecy is implicit in the findings of those scientists who have been studying, and interviewing, dolphins in laboratories. It neither alarms nor surprises me that Nature, whose patience with our self-destructive species is giving out, may have decided to make us, if not extinct, at least a secondary power among the mammals of this improbable planet . . .

As far back as 1933 I observed a school of dolphins (their schools increase as ours decline) romping, as we carelessly call it, alongside a cruise ship in the South Atlantic, and something told me that here was a creature, all gaiety, charm, and intelligence, that might one day come out of the boundless deep and show us how a world can be run by creatures dedicated not to the destruction of their species but to its preservation.

James Thurber, 'Here Come the Dolphins', in *Lanterns and Lances*, New York: Harper and Row, 1961

On the planet Earth, it is estimated that dolphins outnumber human beings two-to-one, and the oceans are hardly overcrowded.

Robert K. G. Temple, *The Sirius Mystery*, London: Sidgwick and Jackson, 1976

It (Orcinus orca) has even been accorded the doubtful honour – along with the wolf in the Soviet Union and the tiger in China – of being subjected to the machinery of modern human warfare. In the summer of 1955, the American air force dropped depth charges on several thousand killer whales off the coast of Iceland after they were accused of destroying fishermen's nets.

Karl-Erik Fichtelius and Sverre Sjölander, *Man's Place: Intelligence In Whales, Dolphins and Humans*, London: Gollancz, 1973

When the mouth is open, it presents a cavity as large as a room, and capable of containing a merchant-ship's jolly-boat, full of men, being 6 or 8 feet wide, 10 or 12 feet high (in front), and 15 or 16 feet long.

W. Scoresby Jnr F.R.S.E., *An Account of the Arctic Regions, with a History and Description of the Northern Whale-Fishery*, Edinburgh: Archibald Constable, 1820

O utside the Antarctic blue whales almost always had empty stomachs . . . thus it appears that blue whales ate for four months and had to go hungry for the next eight.

George L. Small, *The Blue Whale*, New York: Columbia University Press, 1971

W hile no one really believes that Jonah could have lived inside a whale, the one Cetacean stomach he could have entered is that of the Sperm Whale, for both the pharynx and the oesophagus of all other whales are far too narrow to admit a man . . . the Sperm Whale which gulps down thirty-four feet long giant squids could certainly have swallowed Jonah.

E. J. Slijper, *Whales*, London: Hutchinson, 1962

S perm whales feed on squids (Cephalopoda) which have ten arms, eight short and two long ones. They find them everywhere, both in the tropics and in the polar regions, and their stomachs are seldom empty . . . In the Azores Clarke found that the range of size of the squid in the stomachs of the whales he examined was from 2 to 8 feet, while about 3 feet was the average in the tropics and 4½ feet in the Antarctic. At Durban the largest we found was a little over 5 feet, but Clarke saw a specimen of the giant *Architeuthis*, taken from a whale at Horta, Azores, which measured 16 feet 3 inches in standard length and 34 feet in total length from the tip of the body to the tips of the long arms. It weighed 400 lbs. He believes that these giants are swallowed more often than their rarity in the stomachs indicates and thinks that the whales often vomit on being struck by the harpoon, bringing up any large squids they may have swallowed. He actually saw a whale bring one up after being harpooned.

Squids must be very difficult to catch, for they are very agile and alert and can dart out of the way of the largest and fastest net with amazing speed. Nevertheless Sperm whales seem to be capable of devouring them in great quantities, judging by the numbers found in their stomachs, though it is still something of a mystery how they do it.

F. D. Ommanney, *Lost Leviathan*, London: Hutchinson, 1971

M ore than 28,000 squid have been taken from the stomach of one sperm whale.

I. I. Akimusin, 'The feeding of the cachalot', Les Comptes Rendus de l'Academie des Sciences de l'U.R.S.S., 101, pp. 1139–1140, Moscow, 1955

'I t is believed that Sperm Whales do not so much go after this prey as swim about with open mouths, enticing the cuttlefish which seem unable to resist the colourful contrast between the Sperm Whale's purple tongue and white gum of the jaws.' So says E. J. Slijper in his classic book *Whales*, but I have a better explanation of the feeding habits of the sperm whale.

About 18 months ago . . . the technical artist Simon Driver pointed out to me that the sperm whale's lower jaw was uncannily like one of the tentacles of the cuttlefish and squid (especially the giant squid) that they eat. We had been puzzled by the grossly asymmetrical head of the sperm [whale] – why was the lower jaw such a tiny appendage compared with the huge spermaceti-filled head? Could the explanation be that here was a hitherto unreported case of mimicry?

I began to investigate . . . Highly suggestive evidence came to light.

Slijper states: 'Sperm Whales do not chew their food . . . but swallow it whole . . . *Oddly enough* (my italics) the Sperm Whale's exceptionally good set of teeth does not seem to play as important a part in its life as we might have thought. When a young Sperm Whale is weaned and has to look for its own food, the teeth have not yet broken through, and they do, in fact, only appear when the animal has grown to about twenty-five feet, i.e. when it has reached sexual maturity. Moreover, Sperm Whale teeth often show signs of disease or decay and are frequently covered in barnacles, which shows that they are not fully employed.'

If the function of the lower jaw is mainly to resemble the tentacle of a squid, and only secondarily for seizing the cuttlefish, that would explain the sperm whale's retention of teeth where the beaked whales have lost them. The sperm whale is the deepest diver of all the whales; its niche is to dive to prodigious depths, catch its prey with the minimum expenditure of energy, and return to the surface. Deep diving and the tentacular jaw have thus evolved together.

If the mimicry theory is correct, one would expect selection to have produced as narrow a jaw as possible: Slijper draws attention to the degree to which the two halves of the lower jaw are fused into a single narrow bone. The theory does suggest experiment: the behaviour of squid confronted with artificial sperm whale jaws could be investigated. Are the cuttlefish attracted to the jaw and do they attack it; or does the struggle only begin when the whale seizes the squid it has enticed?

Peter Forbes, 'Science and the sperm whale's jaw', *New Scientist*, 21 February 1985

A nother characteristic of the lower jaw is that it can swing out at right angles to the body, not only straight down but also to the sides.

Karl-Erik Fichtelius and Sverre Sjölander, *Man's Place: Intelligence in Whales, Dolphins and Humans*, London: Gollancz, 1973

A whale learns with amazing rapidity, developing such cunning in an hour or two that all a man's smartness may be unable to cope with his newly acquired experience.

Frank T. Bullen. *The Cruise of the 'Cachalot' Round the World after Sperm Whales*, Beccles (Suffolk): Smith Elder, 1898

P erhaps the Sperm Whale is really a genius in disguise; the possibility cannot be totally discounted.

Edward O. Wilson, *Sociobiology: The New Synthesis*, Cambridge, Mass.: Harvard University Press, 1975

G enius in the sperm whale? Has the sperm whale ever written a book, spoken a speech? No, his great genius is declared in doing nothing in particular to prove it.

Herman Melville, *Moby-Dick, or, The Whale*, New York: Harper and Brothers, 1851

I t is interesting to note . . . that especially in the days of sailing ships, whalers reported that sperm-whale herds almost always fled into the wind once they had been frightened. Presumably, this was because sailing ships could not pursue them at an equal speed, since they were forced to tack.

Karl-Erik Fichtelius and Sverre Sjölander, *Man's Place: Intelligence in Whales, Dolphins, and Humans*, London: Gollancz, 1973

T hus authors, we find, of the first respectability in the present day, give a length of 80 to 100 feet, or upwards, to the Mysticetus, and remark, with unqualified assertion, that when the captures were less frequent, and the animals had sufficient time to attain their full growth, specimens were found of 150 to 200 feet in length, or even longer; and some ancient naturalists, indeed, have gone so far as to assert, that whales had been seen of above 900 feet in length.

W. Scoresby Jnr F.R.S.E., *An Account of the Arctic Regions, with a History and Description of the Northern Whale-Fishery*, Edinburgh: Archibald Constable, 1820

There is nothing that reduces man to his proper dimensions more rapidly and completely than contemplation of a fully-grown blue whale at play in the open ocean, and nothing humbles man quite so readily as the sight of one of these animals on land. Man needs no one thing more than humility.

Ivan T. Sanderson, *Follow the Whale*, London: Cassell, 1958

We do not know a great many details, since a school of blue whales is hardly given time to display any of its natural behaviour between the moment it is sighted and the moment the guts of its members are torn to shreds by the tips of an exploding harpoon.

Karl-Erik Fichtelius and Sverre Sjölander, *Man's Place: Intelligence in Whales, Dolphins, and Humans*, London: Gollancz, 1973

A belief of the American whalemen was that the Sperm whale always dies towards the sun, that is, the head, as it rears in the circular path of the flurry, is always directed towards the sun. I have watched the flurry closely in three whales and noticed that this happened on each occasion.

Dr Robert Clarke, 'Sperm Whales of the Azores', *Discovery Reports*, 26, pp. 281–354, Institute of Oceanographic Sciences, University of Cambridge, 1954

A blue whale mortally wounded by several harpoons has been known to tow a modern catcher behind it for two hours before dying.

Paul Budker, *Whales and Whaling*, London: Harrap, 1958

An eighty-foot female blue whale held fast by a modern harpoon head attached to three thousand fathoms of line once towed a ninety-foot, twin-screw steam chaser, with its engines going full speed astern, for seven hours at a steady eight knots, covering over fifty miles without letup.

Ivan T. Sanderson, *Follow the Whale*, London: Cassell, 1958

The weight of a blue whale was of greater significance than was the length because so much of its body was useful to man. Little whales are not worth much, and man usually lets small species live in relative peace. But the blue whale was too big for its own good – it was the prime target. The animal was indeed so big that it was easier to kill than to weigh. How does one weigh an animal whose heart weighs half a ton, whose tongue is bigger than a taxicab, and whose blood supply may exceed 15,000 pints? Several hundred man-hours are required for such a herculean task and no whaling company would willingly waste the labour and the money. Shortly after World War II Japan was permitted by the Commander of the Allied Occupation Forces, General Douglas MacArthur, to rebuild her whaling fleets. He wanted to help the American taxpayer by letting Japan develop the ability to feed herself, but he did require that American inspectors accompany the whalers to enforce compliance with existing international regulations. The Japanese resumed their prewar habit of killing a few undersized whales; when they did so the American inspectors made them weigh a normal-sized whale. The

Japanese quickly learned to obey the rules, but not before they had added significantly to man's knowledge of the weight of whales. Some of their scientists became interested in the subject and they subsequently, and voluntarily, did valuable research on the weight of many species. Of all the tens of thousands of blue whales killed fewer than 30 were ever weighed, about half of which were done reliably by the Japanese. In four representative weighings, the heaviest was a male, No. 1208, whose weight would have surpassed a quarter of a million pounds if it had been possible to weigh his blood which in blue whales represents about 6·5 per cent of its body weight . . . An animal of such staggering proportions is far larger than the largest land animal now alive and statistics on length and weight cannot evoke a true image of its size.

George L. Small, *The Blue Whale*, New York: Columbia University Press, 1971

Whatever the cause of layer formation [in the ear plugs of whales] it is clear from this work that one dark plus one light band represent one year in the life of a Fin whale and that scientists, after thirty years of patient and painstaking research, have arrived at a reliable guide to the age of individual whalebone whales.

In his report Roe (H. S. J. Roe, Discovery Reports, 1967, 35:1–30) reproduces a photograph of a microscopic section of an ear plug of a Fin whale which had eighty layers. Here then, is proof of the longevity of Fin whales at least, for this individual must have been not less than eighty years of age when it was killed.

F. D. Ommanney, *Lost Leviathan*, London: Hutchinson, 1971

Most of us are raised with the belief that man is the most important and most intelligent animal on earth and that we have a very special relationship with the Creator. We believe we are superior to other animals and have a right, even duty, to subdue and use them for our own benefit. As a species we are not accountable to any other on this, 'our' earth. It comes as a surprise and a shock to many of my students when they learn that few animals depend on us, but that we depend on many of them for our continued existence . . .

Every human being has a biological need that must be constantly met – oxygen. And 70% of the oxygen added to the atmosphere each year comes from plankton in the sea. Serious damage to the world ocean therefore could endanger the entire atmosphere of the earth. During the last two decades man has killed so many of the large whales that four species have been rendered commercially as well as almost biologically extinct. These are the blue whale, the fin whale, the humpback and the sei whale. Their population has been reduced from a total of several million to just a few thousand. Every one of these vanished millions of whales used to consume several hundred tons of a large species of zooplankton a year. That plankton now is undergoing a classic population explosion for want of a predator. What will be the effect on the oxygen-producing smaller plankton of the world ocean? What will be the effect on the colour and reflectivity of the oceans? What will be the effect on the average water temperature of the oceans, on its dissolved oxygen content and subsequently on the earth's atmosphere? No one knows. But climatologists know any significant change in ocean temperature can have profound effects on the earth's climates. By killing off the whales of the world man is playing Russian roulette with the earth's primary support system. Yes, we desperately need the whales to preserve the air we breathe.

George Small, Ph.D., College of Staten Island, 'Why Man Needs The Whales', in *Project Interspeak*, ed. T. Wilkes, San Francisco, 1979

Fears of the effects of the devastation of whale herds upon the oxygen supply induced the Governor and State Legislature of Colorado to pass a condemnation of Japanese whaling practices, in 1975, because, in the event of a disruption of the world's oxygen supply, a city like Denver would suffer the most at some 6,000 feet elevation.

Professor George Small of the City University of New York in a letter to Heathcote Williams, 30 November 1987

Thou takest away their breath, and they die, and return to their dust.
Psalms 104:29

Whales do not breathe compressed air but go down with just one lungful, which holds scarcely enough nitrogen to produce problems such as the 'bends', but they avoid the risk of absorbing even this small amount by means of an extraordinary adaptation. As the pressure increases, they simply allow their chests to cave in, so that below 100 m (328 ft) the lungs have collapsed and all the air they contain has been forced into the windpipe and nasal passages where no further nitrogen can be absorbed. Beyond this critical point, they can go on diving in complete safety for as long as they can survive on the oxygen already in their tissues. For the Great Sperm Whale this can mean 90 minutes or more at depths of up to 3,000 m (10,000 ft).

Lyall Watson and Tom Ritchie, *Whales of the World*, London: Hutchinson, 1981

The surface of the body of a large whale, may be considered as comprising an area of 1540 square feet. This, under the common weight of the atmosphere only, must sustain a pressure of 3,104,640 lb., or 1386 tons. But at the depth of 800 fathoms, where there is a column of water equal in weight to about 154 atmospheres, the pressure on the animal must be equal to 211,200 tons. This is a degree of pressure of which we can have but an imperfect conception. It may assist our comprehension, however, to be informed, that it exceeds in weight sixty of the largest ships of the British navy, when manned, provisioned, and fitted for a six month cruise.

W. Scoresby Jnr F.R.S.E., *An Account of the Arctic Regions, with a History and Description of the Northern Whale-Fishery*, Edinburgh: Archibald Constable, 1820

There has been controversy over what actually constitutes the visible blow of a whale. Some say it is simply the warmer air from the lungs forming a vapor as it meets the cooler outside air. Others say it is a foamy mucus, present in the trachea, which is blown out as the animal exhales. A new, more plausible theory is that when the whale rises a small pool of sea water collects just above the blowhole, trapped by the surrounding fleshy ridges. When the whale exhales forcibly, this water is blown away, forming the spout.

Lois King Winn and Howard E. Winn, *Wings in the Sea: The Humpback Whale*, New Hampshire: University Press of New England, 1985

The spout of a Blue whale lasts from three to five seconds and in calm weather a big one may throw up a plume 25 to 30 feet high, rather pear-shaped, widening towards the top.

F. D. Ommanney, *Lost Leviathan*, London: Hutchinson, 1971

The most serious disaster that can befall a cetacean is any incapacity which makes it difficult or impossible to swim and therefore to breathe. Minor injury or concussion, from which a terrestial animal would normally recover, can be fatal for a cetacean. Under these circumstances, it is hardly surprising that most, if not all, species have a powerful, possibly innate, tendency to come to the aid of others in distress. And it is entirely appropriate that this behaviour pattern should involve the simple invariable response of helping an ailing animal to get to the surface.

One of the stimuli which sparks the response seems to be a distress call. There are several accounts of animals coming to the aid of an individual that was clearly out of sight: for example, a report of a group of Great Sperm Whales turning suddenly to go to the side of another which had been harpooned 5 km (over 3 miles) away [F. R. Dulles, *Lowered Boats*, New York: Harcourt, Brace, 1933]. In the days before explosive grenades, the whalers knew that a securely harpooned but not badly injured whale was the best possible lure for enticing others within shooting range. They record that this device worked on all Great Sperm Whales inside a circle with a radius of 6 km [C. H. Robbins, *The Gam*, Boston: Ochs, 1899].

Lyall Watson and Tom Ritchie, *Whales of the World*, London: Hutchinson, 1981

The humpback . . . is particularly well known for its conspicuous mating behaviour, in the course of which the animals leap entirely out of the water and slap each other playfully with their flippers, which makes a sound like artillery fire.

Karl-Erik Fichtelius and Sverre Sjölander, *Man's Place: Intelligence in Whales, Dolphins, and Humans*, London: Gollancz, 1973

In the phenomenon of breaching, when the whale is taking itself almost clear of the water, the flukes will be whistling forty to fifty tons of whale right into the air.

Ronn Storro-Patterson, cited in Ted Crail, *Apetalk & Whalespeak: The Quest for Interspecies Communication*, Los Angeles/Boston: J. P. Tarcher/Houghton Mifflin, 1981

'B reaching' consists of rearing the boiler-like head and trunk far up out of the water, and then falling sideways or backwards with a fine resounding smack which can be heard a long way off. The body has been seen to leave the water altogether in these leaps, and one observer said he saw the setting sun beneath it . . . 'Lobtailing' consists of standing head down more or less vertically in the water and waving the tail from side to side.

F. D. Ommanney, *Lost Leviathan*, London: Hutchinson, 1971

T he whole school surrounded the ship, and performed some of the strangest evolutions imaginable. As if instigated by one common impulse, they all elevated their massive heads above the surface of the sea, and remained for some time in that position, solemnly bobbing up and down amid the glittering wavelets like moveable boulders of black rock. Then, all suddenly reversed themselves, and, elevating their broad flukes in the air, commenced to beat them slowly and rhythmically upon the water, like so many machines.

Frank T. Bullen, *The Cruise of the 'Cachalot' Round the World after Sperm Whales*, Beccles (Suffolk): Smith Elder, 1898

W e have countless reports on this subject – the first dating back to more than 100 years ago. After some introductory love play, whales are said to dive, to swim towards each other at great speed, then to surface vertically and to copulate belly to belly. In so doing, their entire thorax, and often part of their abdomen, as well, are said to protrude out of the water. They then drop back into the sea, with a resounding slap, that can often be heard far away. The authenticity of all the many reports is vouched for by the drawings of one such observation which Nishiwaki and Hiyashi published in 1951.

Similar observations were also made in 1947 by the crew of one of the catchers of the *Willem Barendsz*, by Captain P. G. V. Altveer, Master of the *Eemland* (Royal Dutch Lloyd – 25th September, 1955, off the South American coast between

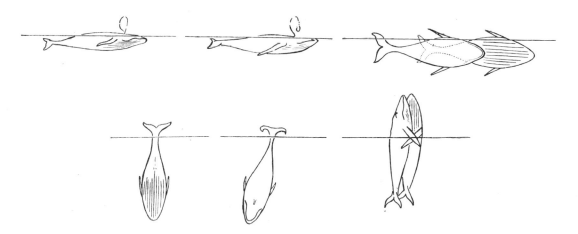

Salvador and Rio de Janeiro), and by Captain H. J. Stiekel, Master of the *Merak N*, who observed courtship in a school of about ten Rorquals at 18°N, and 20°W, on 9th June, 1956. G. Huisken, who served as a stoker on *S.S. Molenkerk*, reports that, in March 1948, on a journey between Karachi and Aden, he observed some members of a school of about 200 Sperm Whales behaving similarly.

E. J. Slijper (Late Professor of General Zoology, University of Amsterdam), *Walvissen*, Amsterdam: D. B. Centen's Uitgeversmaatshappij, 1958

Cetaceans seem to spend an inordinate amount of time in sexual activity. This may be generated by boredom in captivity, but observers in the wild tend to confirm it. Dolphins engage in love-play with almost every creature in sight – with mothers, brothers, fathers, daughters, cousins or aunts. There is even one record of a Bottlenose Dolphin masturbating with a herring (R. Brown, *The Lure of the Dolphin*, Avon: New York, 1979).

A freedom of sexual expression and emancipation of sex from a purely seasonal procreative activity usually indicates a high level of behavioural organization and development. If this is so the sheer quantity as well as the quality, sensitivity and complexity of sexual behaviour in cetaceans puts them very high up the evolutionary tree.

Lyall Watson and Tom Ritchie, *Whales of the World*, London: Hutchinson, 1981

The birth of a humpback probably takes from 25 minutes to two hours . . . Once the calf is born, it cannot breathe underwater because the stimulus for opening the blowhole is air. Without air in its lungs, the calf tends to sink, so the mother may push it to the surface for its first breath . . .

Soon after the calf's birth, the mother expels the placenta. The cetacean placenta, the tissue that attaches the embryo to the wall of the uterus, does not become fused with the mother's tissue. The respective vascular systems are separated by two capillary walls and two epithelial layers. That is why whales do not lose as much blood as humans when they give birth.

The newborn humpback must surface frequently for air, keep warm, and follow its mother. Humpbacks are born with their eyes open, with good hearing, and with the ability to swim. Although the newborn humpback's dorsal fin and flukes are flaccid and do not become rigid for some time after birth, the calf swims easily, if awkwardly, from the moment of birth . . . a myth has it that the tail of the foetus emerges from four to six weeks before birth so that it can practice swimming.

Lois King Winn and Howard E. Winn, *Wings in the Sea: The Humpback Whale*, New Hampshire: University Press of New England, 1985

Samples of blue-whale milk have been chemically analysed on numerous occasions . . . in terms of fat content alone blue-whale milk is about 10 times more concentrated than cows' milk. Part of the explanation for the high fat content is the solution to a biochemical problem facing all whales. As mammals their life processes require a great quantity of water yet never once in their lives can they take a drink. They live in the world's 'driest' climate – salt water. Their water comes from the chemical breakdown of blubber, and the supply of that is limited. Concentrating milk by reducing its water content is one successful measure all whales have adopted for living with a perpetual water shortage.

George L. Small, *The Blue Whale*, New York: Columbia University Press, 1971

A Blue whale foetus, 21 feet in length and weighing 3 tons

The young are already 20 to 23 feet long at birth. They then grow at a prodigious speed, increasing at times by as much as 200 pounds per day in permanent body weight. By the end of seven months the calf is over 50 feet in length, and after two years it is 70 to 75 feet long and, astonishingly enough, sexually mature. We can only speculate as to the causes of this remarkable adaptation, but it is probable that size is the whale's principal protection against various enemies, and that it therefore has to attain this size relatively quickly.

Karl-Erik Fichtelius and Sverre Sjölander, *Man's Place: Intelligence in Whales, Dolphins, and Humans*, London: Gollancz, 1973

Before it was fairly light we lowered, and paddled as swiftly as possible to the bay where we had last seen the spout overnight. When near the spot we rested on our paddles a while, all hands looking out with intense eagerness for the first sign of the whale's appearance. There was a strange feeling among us of unlawfulness and stealth, as of ambushed pirates waiting to attack some unwary merchantman, or highwaymen waylaying a fat alderman on a country road. We spoke in whispers, for the morning was so still that a voice raised but ordinarily would have reverberated among the rocks which almost overhung us, multiplied indefinitely. A turtle rose ghost-like to the surface at my side, lifting his queer head, and, surveying us with stony gaze, vanished as silently as he came.

One looked at the other inquiringly, but the repetition of that long expiration satisfied us all that it was the placid breathing of the whale we sought somewhere close at hand. The light grew rapidly better, and we strained our eyes in every direction to discover the whereabouts of our friend, but for minutes without result. There was a ripple just audible, and away glided the mate's boat right for the near shore. Following him with our eyes, we almost immediately beheld a pale, shadowy column of white, shimmering against the dark mass of the cliff not a quarter of a mile away. Dipping our paddles with the utmost care, we made after the chief, almost holding our breath. The harpooner rose, darted once, twice, then gave a yell of triumph that ran re-echoing all around in a thousand eerie vibrations, startling the drowsy *peca* [fruit-bats] in myriads from where they hung in inverted clusters on the trees above. But, for all the notice taken by the whale, she might never have been touched. Close nestled to her side was a youngling of not more, certainly, than five days old, which sent up its baby-spout every now and then about two feet into the air. One long, wing-like fin embraced its small body, holding it close to the massive breast of the tender mother, whose only care seemed to be to protect her young, utterly regardless of her own pain and danger. If sentiment were ever permitted to interfere with such operations as ours, it might well have done so now; for while the calf continually sought to escape from the enfolding fin, making all sorts of puny struggles in the attempt, the mother scarcely moved from her position, although streaming with blood from a score of wounds. Once, indeed, as a deep-searching thrust entered her very vitals, she raised her massy flukes high in the air with an apparently involuntary movement of agony; but even in that dire time she remembered the possible danger to her young one, and laid the tremendous weapon as softly down upon the water as if it were a feather fan.

So in the most perfect quiet, with scarcely a writhe, nor any sign of flurry, she died, holding the calf to her side until her last vital spark had fled, and left it to a swift despatch with a single lance-thrust. No slaughter of a lamb ever looked more like murder. Nor, when the vast bulk and strength of the animal was considered, could a mightier example have been given of the force and quality of maternal love.

The whole business was completed in half an hour from the first sight of her, and by the mate's hand alone, none of the other boats needing to use their gear. As soon as she was dead, a hole was bored through the lips, into which a tow-line was secured, the two long fins were lashed close into the sides of the animal by an encircling line, the tips of the flukes were cut off, and away we started for the ship . . .

Frank T. Bullen, *The Cruise of the 'Cachalot' Round the World after Sperm Whales*, Beccles (Suffolk): Smith Elder, 1898

In June 1811, one of my harpooners struck a sucker (cub), with the hope of its leading to the capture of the mother. Presently she arose by the 'fast-boat'; and seizing the young one, dragged about a hundred fathoms of line out of the boat with remarkable force and velocity. Again she rose to the surface; darted furiously to and fro; frequently stopped short, or suddenly changed her direction, and gave every possible indication of extreme agony. For a length of time, she continued thus to act, though closely pursued by the boats; and inspired with courage and resolution by her concern for her offspring, seemed regardless of the danger which surrounded her. At length, one of the boats approached so near, that a harpoon was hove at her. It hit, but did not attach itself. A second harpoon was struck; this also failed to penetrate; but a third was more effectual, and held. Still she did not attempt to escape; but allowed other boats to approach; so that, in a few minutes, three more harpoons were fastened; and, in the course of an hour afterwards, she was killed.

There is something extremely painful in the destruction of a whale, when thus evincing a degree of affectionate regard for its offspring, that would do honour to the superior intelligence of human beings; yet the object of the adventure, the value of the prize, the joy of the capture, cannot be sacrificed to feelings of compassion.

W. Scoresby Jnr F.R.S.E., *An Account of the Arctic Regions, with a History and Description of the Northern Whale-Fishery*, Edinburgh: Archibald Constable, 1820

'Killed almost only blue whales today,' a German factory hand, Bruno Schlaghecke, aboard the *Olympic Challenger* wrote in his diary on September 7, 1954, a month before the open season, off the west coast of South America. 'Woe if this leaks out.' Whaling was Bruno Schlaghecke's living, yet the greed of the expedition, the killing of so many small sperm whales, many of which had not even grown teeth, made him feel 'inwardly dumb and empty.' On October 22, he wrote: 'Shreds of meat from the 124 whales killed yesterday are still lying on the deck. Scarcely one of them was full grown. Unaffected and in cold blood everything is killed that comes before the gun.'

The slaughter meant nothing to Ari [Onassis] except in terms of profits and adventure. He never questioned the ethics of the expedition; the whales were there for the taking. It was merely a matter of beating the opposition and grabbing as many as possible. His first expedition in 1950 had netted 'a very nice' $4.2 million. 'Whaling is the biggest dice game in the world,' he said.

Peter Evans, *Ari, The Life and Times of Aristotle Socrates Onassis*, London: Jonathan Cape, 1986

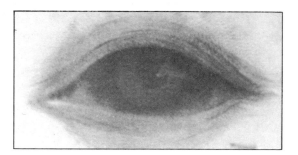

The great, intelligent eyes stared back into his; was it pure imagination, or did an almost human sense of fun also lurk in their depths?

Why were these graceful sea-beasts so fond of man, to whom they owed so little. It made one feel that the human race was worth something after all, if it could inspire such unselfish devotion.

Arthur C. Clarke, *The Deep Range* (Star Science Fiction Stories, ed. Frederick Pohl, No. 3), New York: Ballantine Books, 1954.

The history of the past centuries has been one of successive overexploitation of many of the major whale species. Right, bowhead, gray, blue, humpback and some stocks of fin whales have been depleted to well below their optimum levels. The group affirms that it is not enough to seek protection of a species only after its numbers have been so reduced as to threaten its existence. This minimum action is not resource management. Restraint should be exercised early enough that the species remains sufficiently abundant to fulfil its role in the ecosystem . . .

Reports of Working Groups, *The Whale Problem*, ed. William E. Schevill, Cambridge, Mass.: Harvard University Press, 1974

So little is known about the animals we seem so madly bent on eliminating. Only recently have we become aware of the potential of the toothed whales for rational thought and language. Only recently have we become aware of the importance of the whales as the final elements in the food chain. But for centuries we have known that animals, once extinct, never come back, yet again and again, thanks to the lobbies of greed and a business sense dominated by the myth of Thrasymachus, humans allow the depletion of species to the point of no return.

God knows we have harmed enough things on this planet, but to remove the largest animals God ever made seems to declare an arrogance and shortsightedness that speak volumes more about the intelligence of *homo sapiens* than any great mathematical equation or work of art.

Greg Gatenby, *Whale Sound*, Toronto: Dreadnaught Publications, 1976

Any serious student of abnormal psychology will find 'the whalemen' markedly interesting; it is my own conviction, reached after reading hundreds of log books and sea journals, that the old whaling vessels had more than their arithmetical proportion of madmen.

Capt. Charles B. Hawes, *Whaling*, London: Heinemann, 1924

What is it in our nature that propels us to continue a hunt initiated in earlier times? Are we like some lethal mechanical toy that will not wind down until the last bomb explodes in the last whale's side? What is it that makes so small a thing of eliminating in our lifetime the oceanic role of the largest creature that has lived on our planet? What is it that kills the goose that lays the golden egg? Is it already too late? Is our own obituary scrawled in the fates of the bowhead and right whale, the blue and the humpback – all species that no longer contribute to the biological systems of which they were a part for millions of years? What is the true use of whales beyond bone, beef and blubber?

Scott McVay, 'Reflections on the Management of Whales' (in *The Whale Problem*, ed. William E. Schevill), Cambridge, Mass.: Harvard University Press, 1974

During the night two porpoises came around the boat and he could hear them rolling and blowing. He could tell the difference between the blowing noise the male made and the sighing blow of the female.

'They are good,' he said. 'They play and make jokes and love one another . . .'

Ernest Hemingway, *The Old Man and the Sea*, London: Jonathan Cape, 1951

Coming into existence shortly after the end of a major world war, when the world faced a serious shortage of fats and oils, the Commission was influenced from the start by short-term economic considerations . . . I think all are aware that scientists have been concerned about the effect of whaling on stocks since at least as early as 1910, when the subject was brought up at an International Zoological Congress . . .

From 1945 to 1965 various regulations were in effect on world whaling. It was forbidden to kill some species, prohibitions were in force on killing calves and lactating females, minimum size limits had been set, substantial areas of the world ocean were closed to pelagic whaling, open and closed seasons for whaling had been set, and so on. The Antarctic was the major world whaling area and thus the important regulations were those that applied to the Southern Ocean. But the most important regulation of all in the Antarctic, the blue-whale-unit quota, offered no protection at all to the resource. From the time of the first meeting of the Commission established under the International Convention for the Regulation of Whaling (1946) . . . almost all major actions or failures to act were governed by short-range economic considerations rather than by the requirements of conservation . . .

It is also not understood by many that the International Whaling Commission, in addition to having limited powers to make regulations, has no power at all to enforce them . . . Over and over again the inference is clear that people see the Commission as an irresponsible body, having no power, or not interested in wielding its power, or simply endorsing the wishes of the whaling industry.

J. L. McHugh, 'The Role and History of the International Whaling Commission', in *The Whale Problem*, ed. William E. Schevill, Cambridge, Mass.: Harvard University Press, 1974

With each invention of a better kind of boat and a better kind of spear, the pursuit of whales was carried farther from shore. When at last in the 1860s Svend Foyn perfected the harpoon with a bomb in its head, he opened the last century of whaling. He patented his bomb on Christmas Eve and wrote in his diary. 'I thank Thee, O Lord. Thou alone hast done all.'

Victor B. Scheffer, *The Year of the Whale*, New York: Scribner, 1969

The great era of American whaling, when about 80% of the world catch was taken by American whalers, ended before 1900. The collapse came not from a scarcity of whales, as many people believe, but from the discovery of petroleum in 1859 and destruction of much of the American whaling fleet during the Civil War. The rebirth of whaling in the twentieth century goes back to the invention of the harpoon gun and explosive harpoon head by the Norwegian Svend Foyn in the 1860s; but it was the development of the floating factory in 1903, and especially of the factory ship with stern ramp in 1925, both also by Norwegians, which made expansion into all Antarctic seas possible.

J. L. McHugh, 'The Role and History of the International Whaling Commission', in *The Whale Problem*, ed. William E. Schevill, Cambridge, Mass.: Harvard University Press, 1974

The men had to work over the side, walking about in spike boots on the whale carcasses themselves . . . It was an incredibly wasteful business in those days. Only the blubber was used and the 'skrotts', as the stripped carcasses were called, were cast adrift in the harbour. They floated ashore to rot on the beaches and to this day Deception Harbour, and many of the bays and inlets of South Georgia, are edged with ramparts of bleached bones, skulls, jaws, backbones and ribs, memorials to that uncontrolled slaughter. They bear witness to the greed and folly of mankind. At the shore whaling stations, too, similar profligate waste at first prevailed until the Government intervened to stop it.

F. D. Ommanney, *Lost Leviathan*, London: Hutchinson, 1971

These devices [the pressure cookers] are the basic clue to modern whaling, for without their invention and perfection, the whales could not be processed fast enough to make the whole business pay.

They were invented by a Finnish engineer named Nils Kvaener and act just like vast editions of the housewife's pressure cooker, except that superheated steam under six hundred pounds' pressure is shot into them when they are filled with blubber, meat or other material, and they are then kept running for various lengths of time according to whatever grade of whatever oil is needed . . . The contents, when fully 'cooked', are centrifuged in order to separate the oil from the residue which, in the case of the blubber, is only a little dirty water and useless muck called, like other absolutely worthless parts of the whale, 'grax', but which in the case of the meat and bone cookers consists of various 'meals' that are then dried and bagged. If anything still remains, it is gone over again to take the last drop of oil out of it. Separate boilers handle rare materials like the livers, from which refined vitamin extracts are produced.

Ivan T. Sanderson, *Follow the Whale*, London: Cassell, 1958

Serious pathological conditions are rarely found in whales, as was discovered by a team of six veterinary surgeons and eight assistants led by W. Ross Cockrill. During 1947–1952, this team investigated 12,000 carcasses aboard various factory ships, and had to reject only two because of pathological lesions. 'Whales are probably among the healthiest of living creatures,' he wrote.

Richard Harrison, 'Whales and Whaling', concluding chapter in E. J. Slijper, *Whales*, London: Hutchinson, 1962

Between 170 and 200 of every thousand people who read these lines will die of cancer. That is a peculiarly mammalian disease that spares few species of mammals apart from whales. Cats, dogs, cows, humans and others suffer the scourge of cancer, but not most whales. For example, between 1909 when the killing of blue whales began and 1935 when the killing stopped officially, hundreds and thousands were killed but not one was found with cancer. Was there something in its endocrinal system to prevent it? A clue to a clue? The Japanese and Soviet whalers who killed it to the brink of biological extinction never tried to find out. Now we may never know.

George Small, Ph.D., College of Staten Island, 'Why Man Needs The Whales', in *Project Interspeak*, ed. T. Wilkes, 1979

Only twenty-seven years after the discovery of Alaska the last sea cow was clubbed to death by a hunter in the shallows of the Bering Sea. It weighed perhaps four or five tons and it was the only mammal outside of the tropics that lived on seaweed. We shall never know the secrets of its life: how it survived the freezing winters, how it dealt with the hazards of salty food, what defenses it raised against its enemies, and all the other factors of its body structure and habits. Men will never get insight into the processes of their own lives through study of those of the sea cow.

All species, and in particular the specialized ones – the queer ones – are treasure houses from which man will increasingly draw understanding. In the very *complexity* of the animal lies its great value. No team of engineers, no matter how great the research budget, will ever duplicate a single whisker of a sea cow.

Victor B. Scheffer, *The Day of the Whale*, New York: Scribner, 1969

The penis of a blue whale was six to eight feet long and it was considered amusing to make golf bags out of them.

Sally Carrighar, *Blue Whale*, London: Gollancz, 1978

The pizzle which was formerly used for flogging was, in fact, a bull whale's penis.

E. J. Slijper, *Whales*, London: Hutchinson: 1962

Whaling has played a part in our history that, in certain respects, is second to no other human enterprise, and whale products have been and still are of very great importance to our economy . . . To follow the whale is to follow the whole course of one of the most important and significant aspects of our own history. It is virtually the story of the conquest of our planet.

Ivan T. Sanderson, *Follow the Whale*, London: Cassell, 1958

Man's first contact with these leviathans probably occurred as a result of his coming upon a stranded specimen . . . When ancient man encountered his first whale, it represented a heretofore unimaginable bonanza of meat and oil. It did not take long for early seafarers to realize that it would be more productive to go after the whales, rather than to wait for the whales to come to them. The first whalers were the Basques of what are now the coasts of France and Spain, some time around the year A.D. 1000.

This marked the beginning of what was to become a full-scale, no-holds-barred, mechanized war on the whales . . . Until petroleum was discovered in Pennsylvania in 1858, whales were virtually the sole source of oil for lighting and lubrication . . . European and early American households would have been in total darkness – after the sun had set – until the latter part of the nineteenth century.

Richard Ellis, *Whalewatcher, Journal of the American Cetacean Society*, vol. 20, no. 1, San Pedro, Spring 1986

The mighty whale doth in these harbors lye,
Whose oyl the careful merchant deare will buy.

William Morrell, *New-England, or a briefe Enarration of the Ayre, Earth, Water, Fish, and Fowles of that Country, With a Description of the . . . Habits and Religion of the Natives in Latine and English Verse*, London, 1625

New Plymouth Colony have great profit by whale killing. I believe it will be one of our best returns, now beaver and peltry fail us.

Secretary Edward Randolph, one of the King's Commissioners sent to investigate economic conditions in the American colonies, 1688

During the period 1675–1721 alone they [the Dutch] employed a total of 5886 ships and took 32,907 whales, which, at an average value of almost £900 each, brought a gross of £30,000,000, which in that day and age represented a positively enormous sum of money.

Ivan T. Sanderson, *Follow the Whale*, London: Cassell, 1958

The London market for oil offered rich rewards for colonial whaling. It spurred the American whalers to voyages farther off-shore . . .

By 1748 American whaling had become a powerful factor in colonial trade. It was an established industry, and Nantucket, with its fleet of sixty sail, represented the very heart of the enterprise, its annual catch valued at $96,000.

Thomas Hutchinson, Royal Governor of Massachusetts (1771–74), wrote in his History of Massachusetts that the increase in the consumption of oil by lamps as well as 'divers manufactures' in Europe has been no small encouragement to the colonial whale fishery. 'The flourishing state of the island of Nantucket must be attributed to it', he stated. 'The . . . whale fishery, being the principal source of

our returns to Great Britain, is therefore worthy not only of provincial but national attention.'

Edouard A. Stackpole, *The Sea-Hunters, The New England Whalemen During Two Centuries, 1635–1835*, Westport, Connecticut: Greenwood Press, 1953

The removal of substances from the skin by means of soap seems to have been unknown to the Romans. In Europe up until the seventeenth century, it remained a procedure executed upon the advice of a physician. During the eighteenth century, whale hunting and soap reinforced each other. Soap became cheaper and soap cakes more common.

Soap is the first industrial product to create its own demand and engage the school system as a publicity agent. Development, right into the late twentieth century, has remained associated with water and soap . . .

Only after 1780 was the process of saponification understood scientifically. This made it possible to calculate the quantities of needed ingredients more precisely and to produce soap on a large scale.

Ivan Illich, *H₂O and the Waters of Forgetfulness*, London: Marion Boyars, 1986

Whale oil . . . is used for making candles, margarine and soap.

Pears Cyclopaedia, ed. L. Mary Barker, B.Sc. (London), A. and F. Pears Ltd, Isleworth, Middlesex, 59th edition, Autumn 1949

The ordinary methods of the patent-medicine-man in his pamphlet do have a way of attracting attention and impressing the reader . . . We want to have this hypnotic effect with soap . . . The whole object of advertising is to build a halo around the article. No doubt we shall gradually get to it.

W. H. Lever to John Cheshire, 13 June 1909, cited in Charles Wilson, *The History of Unilever, A Study in Economic Growth and Social Change*, 2 vols, London: Cassell, 1954

Pray, Sir, what in the world is equal to it? Pass by the other parts, and look at the manner in which the People of New England have of late carried on the whale-fishery.

Edmund Burke, *Conciliation with America*, London: J. Dodsley, 1775

The delegates of this Commonwealth . . . impress Congress with just ideas of the high worth and importance of the Whale Fishery to the United States in general and this State in particular.

George Cabot, of the Committee of House and Senate of Massachusetts, 29 October 1782

The first new material to become available was spermaceti. In the last few years of the eighteenth century the whale fishing industry developed rapidly, and of the various species of whale the cachalot or sperm whale was the most prized. When the oil from the head cavity of this creature was cooled, beautiful white crystals were deposited, and these could be separated from the oil by filtering and pressing. The product thus obtained, spermaceti, was found to be a very useful candle material, burning well and of an attractive white translucency.

Still the Candle Burns, printed privately for Price's Patent Candle Company Limited, to record their centenary 1847–1947

CUTTING. UP A WHALE—GATHERING THE SPERMACETI FROM THE HEAD.

The Spermaceti oil gives the clearest and most beautiful flame of every substance known in nature. We are all surprised that you prefer darkness and consequent robberies, burglaries, and murders in your streets to the receiving, as a remittance [for colonial trade], our spermaceti oil. The lamps around Grosvenor Square, I know, and in Downing Street, too, I suppose, are dim by midnight, and extinguished by two o'clock in the morning and chase away, before the watchmen, all the villains, and save you the trouble and danger of introducing a new police into the city.

John Adams, American Minister to England, to William Pitt, May 1785, in *The Works of John Adams*, vol. VIII, p. 309, Boston, 1820

Sperm oil was needed for lighting and heating all over the world . . . and during the middle of the nineteenth century the Yankee Sperm whaling entered upon its golden age . . .

F. D. Ommanney, *Lost Leviathan*, London: Hutchinson, 1971

The whaling interest, taking into consideration the extent to which it has been carried on by our countrymen, may be almost claimed as peculiarly American . . . Our whaling fleet may be said at this very day to whiten the Pacific with its canvas, and the proceeds of this fishery give comfort and happiness to many thousands of our citizens.

Lieut. Charles Wilkes, *Narrative of the United States Exploring Expedition*, vol. 5, Philadelphia, 1845

When information arrived in Hull, Yorkshire, about ships engaged in the whale fishing it would be printed in the local paper, the *Hull Advertiser and Evening Gazette*; details of each ship's catch would be listed individually, but totals would also be given. For example, in 1804 it was published that 24 vessels had returned from Greenland between 20 July and 20 August, and that their total catch comprised 247 whales . . . they had 4,649 butts of blubber, 1,686 tuns of oil and 50½ tons of fins. Sixteen ships had returned from the Davis Strait in the same period with a total catch of 150 whales . . . they had 5,827 butts of blubber, 2,089 tuns of oil and 93½ tons of fins. This made a grand total of 397 whales . . . 10,476 butts of blubber, 3,775 tuns of oil and 144 tons of fins from 40 ships arriving in one month, and gives some idea of the size of the industry.

Thirty tons of oil might be extracted from the blubber of a large whale, and a whale might be worth £2000 in all, the actual amount depending on its size.

The first Hull street directory, published in 1791, shows the following traders associated with the use of whaling products: five candle manufacturers, four stay-makers, one umbrella-maker and one brush-maker, and two firms of oil merchants, one of which was G. and J. Eggington, who were well known as whaling ship owners.

A different picture is provided by the directory for 1826, when the whale fishing industry had reached its peak . . . There were then ten brush-makers, three comb-makers, six soap manufacturers, eight stay-makers, two whale-bone cutters, seven button mould makers, one bristle merchant, eight furriers, sixteen tallow chandlers, six umbrella-makers, seven bone merchants and crushers and fourteen oil merchants . . . all of whom relied at least to some extent on the whale fishery for their material. The comparison shows the extent to which Hull's industry had expanded in the intervening 35 years.

Jennifer C. Rowley, *The Hull Whale Fishery*, Kingston upon Hull: Lockington Publishing Company, 1982

During the period 1835 to 1860 the annual imports of whale products [in America] averaged 117,500 barrels of sperm oil, 25,913 of common whale oil, and 2,323,512 pounds of baleen, valued in all at about eight million dollars of that period, which, of course, had a much greater purchasing power than the dollar of today. Sperm oil was worth 80¢ to $1·62 a gallon, ordinary oil 34¢ to 79¢, and baleen 34¢ to 58¢ a pound. In the peak year of 1846 there were more than seventy thousand men employed in the fleet alone and the vessels were valued at over twenty-two million dollars while the total value of whale products imported reached the colossal figure of seventy million dollars.

America needed oil desperately at that period and was willing to pay handsomely for it . . .

Ivan T. Sanderson, *Follow the Whale*, London: Cassell, 1958

The watchmaker has found himself obliged to fall back on the few, who, for half a century, have supplied with reasonable uniformity oil taken from the head and jaws of the black fish, a species of small whale. This source has proved the most reliable of any for obtaining fine oil, and in proportion to its freedom from adulteration either by foreign admixture, or even by the introduction of oil drawn from other parts of the body of the same fish, is its general excellence and suitability to supply the exacting demands of horology . . .

The process of refining this oil for watch and clock use is slow, requiring fully two years to submit it to all the necessary tests to free it from any tendency to dry or freeze, and to produce that perfect limpidity and quality necessary to withstand the effects of climatic change to which chronometers and watches are subjected on vessels cruising in all latitudes, from arctic seas to tropics. Perhaps the best illustration of the durability of American oils may be found in the chronometers of the New Bedford whalers, which are often absent from home ports from fifty to sixty months upon a voyage, and yet giving the most complete satisfaction, showing on their return traces of oil as fresh as when first supplied.

'J.H.' *Horological Journal*, August 1886

Can he who has discovered only some of the values of whale-bone and whale oil be said to have discovered the true use of the whale? Can he who slays the elephant for his ivory be said to have 'seen the elephant'? These are petty and accidental uses; just as if a stronger race were to kill us in order to make buttons and flageolets of our bones . . .

Henry David Thoreau, *The Maine Woods*, ed. Sophia Thoreau and W. E. Channing, Boston: Ticknor and Fields, 1864

Not only do right whales have the longest whalebone plates (up to 13 feet), but their whalebone is also the strongest and most flexible. These qualities made this whalebone much in demand for use as an elastic element, particularly in corsetry . . . And even if it was possible to take an entire ton of whalebone from a single whale, the market was apparently insatiable.

Female vanity became the ruin of the whale, the same way that the fashion in plumes was once about to exterminate the ostrich, and that the popularity of fur coats today will end in the extinction of the ocelot, the leopard, and the other spotted cats . . .

That the right whales are so splendidly equipped with baleen is probably due to a scantier supply of plankton in their home waters, which means that they must strain more water per unit of food.

Karl-Erik Fichtelius and Sverre Sjölander, *Man's Place: Intelligence in Whales, Dolphins and Humans*, London: Gollancz, 1973

Whalebone has been referred to as 'the plastic of the eighteenth and nineteenth centuries', as it had so many and various uses. Many industries in Hull relied upon it as their raw material. In the Town Docks Museum, Hull, there is a copy of a poster issued by the Whalebone Manufactory, of South Street, Hull . . . Whalebone was also used in ladies' fashions, for stays, hoops, parasols and umbrellas.

Jennifer C. Rowley, *The Hull Whale Fishery*, Kingston upon Hull: Lockington Publishing Company, 1982

The war made whale oil doubly important, not only because supplies of vegetable oils and fats failed, but also because the glycerine in whale oil was at this time a prime necessity for the manufacture of the explosive nitro-glycerine in the armaments industry.

J. N. Tønnessen, and A. O. Johnsen, *The History of Modern Whaling*, trans. R. I. Christophersen, London/Berkeley and Los Angeles: C. Hurst/University of California Press, 1982

S ix thousand blue whales with an average length of 80 feet could produce some 580,000 tons of raw material. From that man could produce 105,000 tons of oil, enough to supply 2·5 ounces of margarine or edible oil every day for a year to 4,138,000 adult human beings . . . The recorded kill of blue whales in the Antarctic from 1909 to 1935 was 328,177.

George L. Small, *The Blue Whale*, New York: Columbia University Press, 1971

I n March 1916 under the Defence of the Realm Regulation 30A, the Ministry of Munitions prohibited all dealings in whale oil without licence. Whale oil was the cheapest source of glycerine supply. Almost all the whale oil in the world was obtained from British territorial waters in the Antarctic, although whaling was mainly carried out by Norwegians. The whole supply was secured by appending to the licences issued for whaling in British waters a condition that the oil should be brought to a port of call in the United Kingdom and sold in the United Kingdom. Arrangements were made in February 1916 to take over the businesses of certain leading whale oil merchants to act as agents for the Ministry of Munitions. A good stock of raw material had accumulated in 1916. In February 1917 a separate department of the Explosive Supply Department was formed to deal with the supply of whale oil. A reduction in gun ammunition production in February 1918 reduced the demand.

History of the Ministry of Munitions, volume 7: 'The control of materials', part 4: 'Materials for explosives manufacture' (originally issued for confidential use only), London: HMSO, 1921

I t was here [in South Africa] that Lever Brothers (from 1930 Unilever Ltd.) commenced active participation in whaling. Its keenest rival in the South African fat market was the New Transvaal Chemical Co., which in 1912 had added whaling, based on two stations, to its many and varied enterprises. William Lever (created Lord Leverhulme in 1917) pursued his customary policy as far as this new rival was concerned: if he could not crush the rival, then he would buy him, and this was in fact done in 1914, for a very high price, £135,000 being paid for the whaling company alone.

When Lord Leverhulme bought the Southern Whaling & Sealing Co., in 1919, and commenced operations from the Hebrides in 1923, he was greatly interested in the production of whale meat . . . and in 1924 he started his own company, the Ocean Harvest Co., for the purpose of marketing fresh meat to the natives of Africa as well as all other products of the whale apart from oil . . . but interest in it dropped as soon as the price of oil rose again.

When the keystone to this empire was finally fitted into position on 2 September 1929 with a merger between Margarine Unie and Lever Bros. to form Unilever Ltd., practically all other buyers were shut out from the whale oil market . . . The struggle for whale oil had been an important motive for the amalgamation that produced Unilever Ltd . . .

Proof was available that no one overfished that season 1931–2 to the extent that Unilever's expeditions did. The Norwegian Whaling Council expressed the opinion current in Norway with regard to British whaling policy: 'Britain's interest in preserving stocks of whale is undoubtedly considerable, but when her own interests are concerned, she withdraws. Britain is not prepared to sacrifice a penny of her own interests.'

Unilever regarded 1·8 million barrels as their minimum annual requirement [for Port Sunlight]. As there were few sales outside Unilever, there was no need for the other whaling companies . . .

Now that warehouses were full, factories were ordered to step up the use of whale oil in soap and margarine, particularly the latter, and as a result only some 75,000 tons was earmarked for other products. Even in Sunlight soap, the recipe for which no one had dared to alter, 20 per cent of hydrogenated whale oil was now used without consumers noting any change of quality. In short, as D'Arcy Cooper (Lord Leverhulme's successor) declared in July 1930, 'The interests of the Family as a whole might require more whale oil to be used.'

Documents submitted at the War Crimes Tribunal in Nuremburg reveal that the German economy, from as far back as the summer of 1933, was based on war. In May of that year Hitler appointed a highly secret Reich Defence Council, in which Hjalmar Schacht was the supreme authority and Wohlthat [Ministerial Direktor in the Reich Economics Ministry, Helmuth C. H. Wohlthat] his right hand . . . In the Defence Council Wohlthat was active, on the highest level, in fitting whale oil into the German war economy . . .

The *Völkischer Beobachter*, mouthpiece of the National Socialist Party, had announced that Germany would construct ten whaling expeditions . . . The experience of the First World War had shown that in a new war supplies of fat would prove Germany's Achilles' heel. Chamberlain had stated that it was less important for Britain to secure whale oil than to prevent Germany getting it . . .

Hitler's decree of 20 March 1933 provided a dramatic conclusion to the measures initiated, clearly aimed at preparing for a wartime economy. All bakeries and restaurants were compelled to display notices clearly informing the public that whale oil was used in the margarine . . .

The announcement that the German Government had decided to build a German whaling fleet and was anxious for Unilever's cooperation, had an immediate effect on the price . . . In April [1935], 63,400 tons were sold to Germany for £15.10s., and later that month Unilever bought 30,000 tons at a rate of £14.10s. on behalf of the German Government. All the oil for 1934–5 was thus accounted for . . .

In the summer of 1935 Unilever contemplated building three floating factories in Germany . . . Wohlthat pointed out that as the whale oil reaching Germany was quite insufficient for Unilever, 'the company was forced by the currency situation to start whaling under the German flag, so that they could obtain the raw material they required . . .'

In 1935, 32 per cent of all ships in German yards were being built on Unilever's account, formally for its Dutch subsidiary, Unilever N.V. In April 1937 Wohlthat declared that Germany would require 200,000 tons of the 1937–8 production, and she acquired exactly this amount in 1938 . . .

Two objects had been achieved: the German fat market had been relieved of pressure from the world fat market, and Germany's agriculture had been rescued from economic collapse. 'Had Germany in 1914 had 300,000 tons of whale oil, the shortage of fats would never have been so menacing,' was how the propaganda put it.

Having acquired a new whaling fleet under the German flag, the Nazis naturally concealed the fact that this was being done with Dutch–British capital. At the general meeting of Unilever in 1938 D'Arcy Cooper pointed out that of the four German expeditions operating in 1937–8, one, the *Unitas*, was entirely owned by

Unilever, while in the others it had interests of 50 per cent or more. To quote Goering on the subject of German whaling, foreign capital and whalers 'offer the possibility of supporting the supply of fats to our people, and thereby contributing to the attainment of the great goal of freedom in raw materials and food'. In other words: they were helping Germany to set up her wartime economy.

J. N. Tønnessen, and A. O. Johnsen, *The History of Modern Whaling*, trans. R. I. Christophersen, London/Berkeley and Los Angeles: C. Hurst/University of California Press, 1982

Holt [S. J. Holt, *Food and Agriculture Organisation Report*, 1976, ACMRR/MM/SC/7] has calculated the total weight of the annual world catch of whales from 1910 to 1973. From a few thousand tons prior to the development of the Antarctic pelagic fishery it rose to just over 3 million tons in 1938, the year the Antarctic catch reached its peak. It remained steady at about 2·3 million tons from 1949 to 1962.

K. Radway Allen, *Conservation and Management of Whales*, Division of Marine Resources, Seattle: University of Washington Press, 1980

The 1945 Potsdam Agreement prohibited the Germans from building any ship over fifteen thousand tons . . . As well as being prohibited from building big ships, Germany had been outlawed by the Allies from redeveloping its prewar whaling fleets. So not only was there a gap in a very lucrative market, but Gratsos had discovered that the Potsdam Agreement put no limit on conversion work. Ari could use the German yards to convert an eighteen-thousand-ton tanker into a floating factory ship . . .

In a befuddling nest of deals, the factory ship *Olympic Challenger* (formerly the T2 tanker *Herman F. Whiton*), financed by a corporation controlled by an Argentinian citizen and affiliated to American Pacific Tankers Inc. in New York, was transferred to a company registered in Panama and run by the Olympic Whaling Company in Montevideo, Uruguay. Significantly, neither Panama nor Uruguay had signed the 1946 Washington Convention, which had decreed a maximum quota of sixteen thousand whales a season. The *Challenger*'s seventeen catcher ships flew Honduran and Panamanian flags, although the commander and most of the 519 seamen were German. The expedition manager was the Norwegian-born Lars Andersen, said by many whalers to be one of the greatest harpoonists of all time. A Nazi collaborator (he stood trial after the war and was fined $160,000), he was advising Juan Perón on Argentina's whaling fleet when Ari caught up with him in Buenos Aires. 'He's tough, expensive, unpleasant and an unscrupulous sonofabitch,' Ari told Gratsos. 'Just like me – only with a harpoon!'

Ari believed that, like war in the mid-nineteenth century, when generals and their ladies had picnicked on a Sebastopol hillside to watch the charge of the Light Brigade, whaling was a spectator sport, and as he sipped hot toddies with his guests, the gunners made use of their grenade harpoons with a terrible diligence. A broad cloak of blood extended over the surface of the sea. The *Olympic Challenger* was the first factory ship to use a helicopter to seek out its prey; it hovered surreally in the air like a hawk. Some of his guests had been to fiestas in Rio and to grand balls in Venice; none of them had been to anything like this. Only Ari, it was agreed, would think of organizing a whale hunt in the Antarctic Ocean. The men were invited to try their skill with the harpoon gun. 'I think he simply wanted them to feel the blood on their hands and share the guilt,' Gratsos said later . . .

Ari did not hide the fact that he was aroused by the spectacle of cruelty; 'For Tina I'm sure the hunt evoked a pleasurable psychic high,' said a close woman companion. Later Ari talked of the 'predatory satisfaction' the warmth of Tina's body gave him beneath the soft white crêpe nightgowns she always wore aboard the *Challenger*.

Peter Evans, *Ari, The Life and Times of Aristotle Socrates Onassis*, London: Jonathan Cape, 1986

A whale is often referred to as a 'treasure house of pharmaceuticals' because of its incomparable size and complicated and delicate body structure. Take, for example, certain animal hormones used to treat illnesses. The amounts of such hormones that can be extracted from cattle or horses are minimal whereas one whale can supply hormones equivalent to those of one hundred horses. So, from time to time, whalers comply with requests of pharmaceutical companies to keep certain whale organs.

In 1935, a doctor travelling with a Norwegian fleet named Jacobsen detected a hormone from a whale's pituitary gland that affected human blood pressure, uterine contraction, urinal secretion, etc. He also successfully isolated a hormone that adjusted human growth, secretion of the thyroid gland and sexual functions. In the wake of Jacobsen came Philip Hench of Norway and other doctors who extracted an anterior pituitary hormone that stimulates the adrenal cortex, for which they received the Nobel prize shortly after the end of World War II. This medicine, called ACTH, is particularly helpful in the treatment of arthritis and rheumatism. At one time, with the cooperation of a whaling fleet, 180 kilograms of pituitary glands were collected and 25,000 ampoules of ACTH were distributed to hospitals free of charge.

Morikuni Itabashi, *Pharmaceuticals from Whales, A Brief Whaling Perspective*, Tokyo: Japan Whaling Association, 1986

Insulin extracted from the whales' pancreases in large volume is effectively used for treating diabetics, whose numbers are said to be rising. Such 'seeds' for new medicines are almost everywhere in the whale's body, including the thyroid gland, adrenal glands and liver, on which various research is still being undertaken. These hormones, however, become ineffective unless the organs are taken out of the whale's body immediately after its death, compelling flensers to work quickly and to freeze the organs right away. Whale hormones are indeed the ambergris of the modern age.

Morikuni Itabashi, *Pharmaceuticals from Whales, A Brief Whaling Perspective*, Tokyo: Japan Whaling Association, 1986

Ambergris, or grey amber, is a light, inflammable, fatty substance, ashy grey in colour, but when cut through it shows a sort of marbling. It has a pleasant aroma, especially when heated, and this is due to the presence of a bacterium with the name of *Spirillum recti physeteris*. Ambergris is formed in the large intestines of sperm whales, apparently as the result of ulceration caused therein by irritations set up by the horny beaks and bony rings from the suckers of the squids the whales eat. It is one of the most valuable fixatives for our highest-priced perfumes. Ambergris has fetched a price of £143 an ounce.

Ivan T. Sanderson, *Follow the Whale*, London: Cassell, 1958

Whalemeat was introduced into Britain in 1947, when disagreements with the Argentine were making it difficult to augment the dwindling home meat supplies. Whalemeat was a curious powdery-textured substance resembling a meaty biscuit, with overtones of oil. But it had a fair success. By September 1947 Lyons were serving six hundred whale steaks a day at one London Corner House, and the Caterers' Association were observing, with enthusiasm and some relief, that 'the public will take all we can give them, especially now the meat ration is cut.'

Since a single blue whale weighs about ninety tons, the Ministry of Food found this joyful news. Vast refrigerated ships were despatched to the Antarctic, and whalemeat became familiar on butchers' slabs. By 1949 it was arriving in tins; described by the shippers as 'rich and tasty – just like beef steak.'

Michael Sissons and Philip French, *Age of Austerity, 1945–1951*, London: Hodder and Stoughton, 1963

Whalemeat had the advantage that, coming from South Africa, it could be paid for in sterling instead of dollars. Imported in ninety-ton carcasses on board refrigerated ships, it proved to be cheap and acceptable, if not exactly popular.

Professor Magnus Pyke was Principal Scientific Officer at the Ministry of Food when whalemeat was introduced:

They brought some whalemeat to the UK and butchered it and I got a lovely slab of about six pounds of whale steak . . . we cut it off and we grilled it and when we served it out and looked at this lovely chump of juicy steak, our mouths were drooling. You put it in your mouth and you'd start biting it and it tasted like steak, and then as you went on biting it the taste of steak was suddenly overcome by a strong flavour of – cod liver oil.

As a housewife, Mrs Vera Mather tried whalemeat but regretted the experiment:

The only thing I can say about whalemeat is that there was a lot of it and it was very smelly, terribly smelly and it didn't taste like anything, it was neither fish nor meat. I think we had it once in our house but you could smell it right through the house for the whole week afterwards.

Whalemeat received a mixed press but was tolerated for two or three years for want of anything better . . . Visitors to Butlins Holiday Camps had, of course, to take their food ration books and hand them over to the management for the coupons to be clipped out. Later, they might have to sit down to a whalemeat dinner.

Paul Addison, *Now the War Is Over: A Social History of Britain, 1945–51*, London: Jonathan Cape/BBC Publications, 1985

European whalers could not sell whale meat in their home markets simply because people would not eat it. Several promotional campaigns were apparently made to stimulate the sale of whale meat in several European companies, but without success. The Norwegian company Kosmos A/S did succeed in developing in 1961 an outlet for whale meat as pet food in the United Kingdom. Although the Kosmos company did in its annual report divulge the name of the English purchaser, Petfoods Ltd., they would not tell me the price they received. The reason for this is not known since the price of all other important products was divulged. It may have been kept secret for fear that knowledge of substantial profit based on pet food at the risk of exterminating the blue whale might arouse moral condemnation of the company, I was, however, able to learn the price received by Kosmos for the whale meat it sold for pet food. The information came from an employee of the company who was morally disgusted by this and other practices of his employer. In 1961 the price per ton was £75 and by 1967 it had risen to £100. The Kosmos company enjoyed a great advantage in this market for its whale meat, and in some of its annual reports it admitted as much. It did not admit, naturally, that profits were being maintained at the risk of biological extinction of the blue whale that was being killed to feed dogs and cats in England.

George L. Small, *The Blue Whale*, New York: Columbia University Press, 1971

The importance to the Japanese whaling companies of their production of whale meat is so great that it can hardly be overemphasized. The production and sale of whale meat was almost exclusively Japanese because only in that nation did the culinary habits of the Japanese create a substantial market for it. This was a distinct economic advantage to the Japanese whaling companies because a significant portion by weight of a blue or other baleen whale consisted of meat that yielded little oil. During the 1950s their production of whale meat at domestic land-based whaling stations alone exceeded that of all non-Japanese companies operating pelagically in the Antarctic. By 1960 total Japanese production of whale meat exceeded 155,000 tons and was greater than her domestic production of beef from cattle.

The peak of production came in 1964/65 when Antarctic operations alone produced 147,721 tons. Most of this production was frozen and sold as a competitor and substitute for beef, but at one-third the price.

George L. Small, *The Blue Whale*, New York: Columbia University Press, 1971

The uniqueness of whale cuisine in Japan has been that almost every part of a whale is prepared and served. Let alone red meat, the Japanese have eaten tailmeat, skin, blubber, and tongue, and even prized such delicacies as gums (called kohige), lungs (fukiwata), spleen (ikawata), small intestines (hyakuhiro), kidneys (mamewata), penis (takeri), and the cartilaginous part of the nose (kaburabone). The last one on this list, in particular, was highly valued as a rare delicacy, and is now sold in cans in the Kyushu region.

Morikuni Itabashi, *Culinary Abundance, A Brief Whaling Perspective*, Tokyo: Japan Whaling Association, 1986

Six thousand blue whales with an average length of eighty feet could produce 189,000 tons of meat, enough for a 6-ounce steak every day for a year for 3,090,000 adult human beings.

George L. Small, *The Blue Whale*, New York: Columbia University Press, 1971

Nearly all baleen whale meat is tender, making it an excellent food. Meat that is sold fresh on the market comes from coastal whaling operations whereas all mother-ship products arrive in Japan in frozen form. Though frozen whale-meat once had a reputation for being rather unpalatable, it is now just as acceptable as fresh whalemeat, thanks to the development of rapid freezing technology.

The most famous cut of whalemeat is 'onomi' tailmeat that comes from the base part of the tail. This cut is equivalent to a fillet of pork and beef, and is primarily used for sashimi, thinly sliced and eaten raw dipped in flavoured soy sauce, and for broiled steaks. Since tailmeat constitutes only a small portion of the whale, and because it tastes so good, this cut fetches the highest prices on the market.

'Akaniku' (red meat) is the cut which comes mainly from the whale's back and belly, and is most common. This cut is used for sashimi and grilling, as well as for processing into reconstituted hams, sausages and canned meat. 'Kogire' denotes tiny scraps of meat obtained by scraping edible meat from tendons and bones. This practice indicates how exhaustively whales are used by the Japanese.

'Munaniku' (breast meat) is slightly tougher than red meat, and is usually sliced thin and grilled, or mixed into reconstituted hams. 'Abura-sunoko', the streaky meat from the base of the pectoral fins, is sold for the price of red meat, and is particularly delicious when sliced thin and cooked as sukiyaki.

'Kanoko' is the meat that covers the lower jawbone, in which numerous spots of red meat are embedded in fat. This cut is highly valued because of the relatively small amounts per whale.

'Une' and 'sunoko' both come from the furrows that run from the lower jaw to the belly of baleen whales. The portion from the skin through the blubber is called 'une', and the tender meat beneath it is referred to as 'sunoko'. The former is eaten salted, while the latter is for canned, cooked meat. The unseparated cut of 'une' and 'sunoko' is processed into whalemeat bacon.

Blubber is often eaten, as well as squeezed for its oil. The Japanese even eat the skin and certain parts of the tail fin of baleen and sperm whales!

Morikuni Itabashi, *Whalemeat as Food, A Brief Whaling Perspective*, Tokyo: Japan Whaling Association, 1986

The use of higher fatty acid contained in whale oil is expanding rapidly; from margarines and detergents to plasticizers and synthetic polymerization regulators. From hormones to the chemical industry, uses for whales seem endless. A whale is probably the largest single source – in the literal sense of the word – for pharmaceuticals and organic chemicals.

Morikuni Itabashi, *Pharmaceuticals from Whales, A Brief Whaling Perspective*, Tokyo: Japan Whaling Association, 1986

THE MANY USES OF WHALES

The whale is the largest animal in the world. Not only is a great deal of oil and meat obtained from its body, but every part of it can be used to the benefit of our lives.

鯨はこんなに役にたつ

鯨は地球上で一番大きな動物です。その体からは、たくさんの油や肉がとれるのをはじめ、すみずみまで役にたって、私たちの生活を豊かにしてくれます。

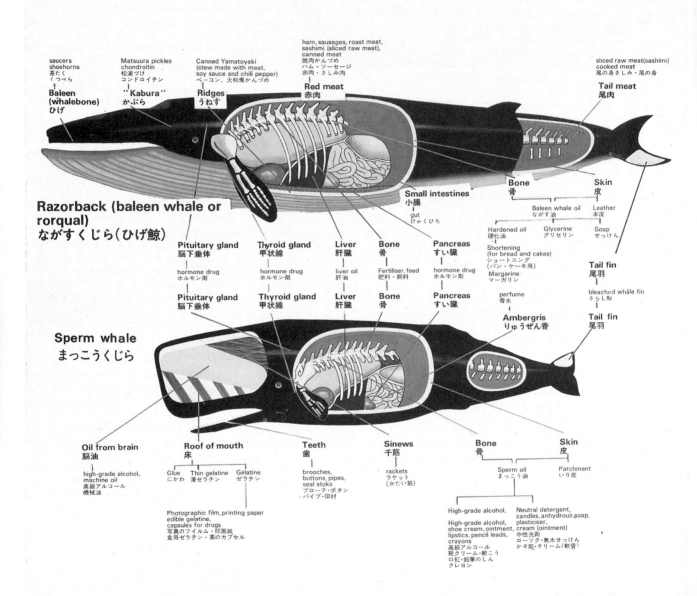

To their credit, the Japanese don't waste anything, unless you consider killing an animal a total waste. They do use all parts of the whale. The oils are used for rocketry or for oil for automobile transmissions in automobiles. Bones are ground up into fertilizer.

. . . the Soviet Union takes whales primarily as a source of foreign currency. Sales of whale meat to Japan provides yen, which the Soviets desperately need. Iceland and South Korea sell their catches to Japan too.

Maxine McCloskey, former U.S. delegate to the International Whaling Commission, Whale Centre Newsletter, vol. 7, no. 3, Oakland, California, 1984

Regarding the technical use of Sperm Oil, I feel it might be worth reiterating the oil industries' former involvement with this particular product.

Until the 1960s, Sperm Oil was used by most of the major oil companies as an additive in both soluble and neat metalworking oil.

Metalworking oil is, as you may know, used as a medium through which cutting operations (on metal and similar hard substances) take place. There is, therefore, a tenuous link between Sperm Oil and virtually all manufactured goods (where metal is involved) produced.

Extract from a letter to Heathcote Williams from G. F. Wheeler, Publicity Executive, Burmah-Castrol (U.K.) Limited, 8 August 1986

The average sperm [whale] yields more oil (65 to 80 barrels) than even the mighty blue whale of equal bulk (50 to 70 barrels) . . . the spermaceti, which is really a very light wax – a neutral, almost tasteless, fatty substance which is a liquid between thirty-eight and forty-seven degrees centigrade – is not only suitable for the manufacture of candles, for which it was mostly used in olden days, but also forms the basis of some of the finest machine oils known for very delicate instruments . . .

Ivan T. Sanderson, *Follow the Whale*, London: Cassell, 1958

What is spermaceti oil for? In the sperm whale's head is a huge cavity filled with this extremely fine oil which, until recently, was used as a transmission oil in Rolls-Royces and earlier was used for the smokeless spermaceti candles. It is a yellow oil which hardens in the air into a whitish wax. The cavity, called the case, in a bull whale is about 5 feet deep and 12 feet long, and contains up to ten barrels of oil. It is generally accepted that in part the case serves as an echo-location and communication system. Most cetaceans have some such cavity. Dolphins have a fatty area called a melon, which is believed to serve the same purpose. However, in the sperm whale the size is so vast that some other purpose is thought to be involved.

Soviet scientist V. A. Kozak in 1974 introduced a 'third eye' concept that makes the whale sound like it has its own indoor motion picture theatre. This theory suggests that the spermaceti organ works as a 'video-acoustic system' which transfers sound energy into images, using the rear wall of the case as an 'acoustic retina'. More interesting, however, and bringing us back to the riddle of how the whale feeds itself, is the Flash Gordon-style 'stun-ray' theory. Two other Soviets, U. M. Belkovich and A. V. Yabalkov, in 1963 proposed that the spermaceti organ is used to focus a shock wave, a kind of projected sonic boom, to stun its prey. It was 'an effective instrument for stunning and immobilizing prey far away'. Too space-age? Not according to the Israeli study of A. A. Berzin, who in 1972 supported the Russian conclusions and wrote: 'When mobile squid and fish are discovered, the ultrasonic beam narrows and focuses on them, its frequency sharply increases, and the prey is stunned and seized.'

More recent dolphin research at the University of California at Santa Cruz by

Ken Norris and Ken Martin in 1985 tends to support this stun-ray theory. Also, recordings have been made of sperm whales using what is believed to be this high-intensity, low-frequency blast of sound. The blasts are intense rather than loud, and to the human ear sound like rifle shots fired over the clicking echo-location sounds that are used to scan for victims. Tests indicate that fish or squid subjected to the full force of the blasts would not just be stunned but would have parts of their body tissue destroyed, and would quite likely be killed. (Music, no doubt, to the American military. Let no one be surprised if the Pentagon is already at work on some sort of underwater star wars laser system.)

David Day, *The Whale War*, London and New York: Routledge and Kegan Paul, 1987

Cetaceum (spermaceti). A concrete fatty substance obtained from the head of the sperm whale, separated from the admixed sperm oil by freezing and hydraulic pressure. When refined with dilute caustic soda solution it becomes almost neutral. Spermaceti has a lustrous crystalline structure, consists almost entirely of cetyl palmitate (cetin), and melts about 45°. It is of value in the manufacture of both liquid and solid creams; also used in lipsticks.

W. A. Poucher, *Perfumes, Cosmetics and Soaps*, vol. 1 'The Raw Materials of Perfumery', revised by George M. Howard, Eighth Edition, London: Chapman and Hall, 1979

Though it is said that science provides substitutes, it will be a long time before whale oil is completely replaced by synthetics. Whale oil is indeed a 'treasure box' of organic chemistry . . . Sperm oil makes excellent antifreeze lubricant for cars, and is even used in the engines of space rockets and missiles.

Morikuni Itabashi, *Civilization's Torch, A Brief Whaling Perspective*, Tokyo: Japan Whaling Association, 1986

Computer print-out of current NASA abstracts relating to the properties of Sperm Whale oil as a lubricant:

```
82N10134 NASA STAR    Issue 01
   Heterogeneous  electron transfer kinetic parameters of hemeproteins as studied
by channel flow hydrodynamic voltammetry  / Ph.D. Thesis
   (AA)CASTNER, J. F.
   Virginia Commonwealth Univ., Richmond.  (V0181760)
   810000  p. 129  In: EN (English)  Avail: Univ. Microfilms  Order No. 8118962
p.21

   The  technique  of channel flow hydrodynamic voltammetry was used to elucidate
the  heterogeneous  electrochemical  behavior  of  the hemeproteins myoglobin and
cytochrome.  Sperm  whale myoglobin was principally studied due to its stability
and  availability even though physiologically this hemeprotein does not function
as an electron transporting agent. A methyl viologen modified Au foil electrode
was  used  in this investigation. The modified electrode surface facilitated the
reversible  reduction  and  oxidation  of  myoglobin  as was demonstrated by the
technique  of  spectroelectrochemistry. Channel flow hydrodynamic voltammetry
provided  rapid attainment of steady state reaction conditions which resulted in
the acquisition of precise kinetic measurements.
Dissert. Abstr.
   Category code: 25 (inorganic/physical chemistry)
```

```
   MYOGLOBIN ADSORPTION ONTO CROSSLINKED POLYDIMETHYLSILOXANE
   Darst, Seth A.; Robertson, Channing R.; Berzofsky, Jay A.
   Stanford Univ, Stanford, CA, USA
   J  Colloid  Interface  Sci  v  111  n  2  Jun  1986, Symp  on  Protein  and
Polyelectrolyte Adsorpt, Potsdam, NY, USA, Jun 24-25 1985 p 466-474 Coden:
JCISA ISSN: 0021-9797  In ENGLISH  Refs: fs
   Doc. Type: JOURNAL ARTICLE

   The  adsorption  of  sperm whale myoglobin (Mb) on crosslinked
polydimethylsiloxane (silicone rubber) from flowing solutions is examined using
total  internal  reflection  fluorescence (TIRF). By comparing the experimentally
observed  relationship  between the adsorption rate and the wall shear rate with
the  predictions  of a convection/diffusion model, it is shown that the initial
adsorption  is  diffusion-controlled over the observed range of wall shear rates
(49 to 410 s**-**1). (Edited author abstract) 38
```

Obtained from the European Space Agency, 8–10 rue Mario-Nikis, 75738 Paris, September 1986

I decided to act on the whales. The showdown came with representatives of the State Department and the Sperm Oil industry. When I had disposed of the majority of their arguments, they produced an argument I had not expected. 'We have to have whale oil for the space program,' the State Department official declared.

Without hesitation I demanded, 'What are you going to use when the whale is extinct?'

Taken aback, the official stammered, 'I suppose we'll have to find a substitute.'

Walter J. Hickel, former Governor of Alaska, and ex-Secretary of the Interior, *Who Owns America?* New Jersey: Prentice-Hall, 1972

The teeth [of the sperm whale] lack enamel, and are used industrially in the same way as ivory – for buttons, piano keys, markers in games, and so forth.

Karl-Erik Fichtelius and Sverre Sjölander, *Man's Place: Intelligence in Whales, Dolphins and Humans*, London: Gollancz, 1973

The motor launch skipper, Antonio José, said that 'The whale teeth are being smuggled into a country which prohibits them.' Locally a number of teeth are sold from the basement workshop of Othon Silveira . . . He states that he purchased all the teeth from the 1984 hunt and that he has a stock of over half a ton. He pays around $90 a kilo for the teeth.

Nick Carter and Allan Thornton, *Pirate Whaling 1985 and a History of the Subversion of the International Whaling Regulations*, London: Environmental Investigation Agency, 1985

Othon Silveira poses with part of his half-ton stock of whale teeth, July 1984, Horta, Faial, Azores

Seizing his sharp boat-spade, he commenced an excavation in the body, a little behind the side fin. You would almost have thought he was digging a cellar there in the sea . . . Dropping his spade, he thrust both hands in, and drew out handfuls of something that looked like ripe Windsor soap, or rich mottled old cheese; very unctuous and savory withal. You might easily dent it with your thumb; it is of a hue between yellow and ash color. And this, good friends, is ambergris, worth a gold guinea an ounce to any druggist . . . Ambergris is soft, waxy, and so highly fragrant and spicy, that it is largely used in perfumery, in pastiles, precious candles, hair-powders, and pomatum. The Turks use it in cooking, and also carry it to Mecca, for the same purpose that frankincense is carried to St Peter's in Rome. Some wine merchants drop a few grains into claret, to flavor it.

Who would think, then, that such fine ladies and gentlemen should regale themselves with an essence found in the inglorious bowels of a whale!

Herman Melville, *Moby-Dick, or, The Whale*, New York: Harper and Brothers, 1851

Pilot whales are routinely victims of the notorious Icelandic ritual slaughter known as the *grind*, which exploits the tendency of the pod to follow a leader (or pilot). In the *grind* the leader is diverted into shallow waters; the pod follows and all are then hacked to death with ceremonial knives and the meat distributed according to ancient formulae.

The Times, London: 30 October 1986

Perhaps the strangest method of whaling was that used in a fjord near Bergen, Norway, at the beginning of this century. Here Fin and Sei whales were driven into a narrow fjord the entrance to which was closed by means of a net drawn across it so as to entrap the whale. It was then assailed with lances which had been dipped in the putrefying flesh of previously killed whales. In a few days the victim died in the fjord from gangrene – a barbarous way of killing an animal for commerce.

F. D. Ommanney, *Lost Leviathan*, London: Hutchinson, 1971

Each year hundreds of Pilot whales are killed in a very brutal manner by locals in the Faroe Islands. A record number of 2,973 were killed in 1981.

The kill itself is very inhumane, indiscriminate and savage. Using small boats the Pilot whales are driven into a small bay from which they cannot escape. They are then driven onto the beach or gaffed using scythe-like hooks.

When the whales are caught, the hunters begin to saw, using a large knife, across the whale's back at a point behind the blowhole until the spinal column is exposed and unprotected by muscle tissue. The subsequent thrashing of the whale, which is obviously in great pain, causes the animal to die by snapping its spinal column. Because sometimes as many as 500 whales can be killed at one time, taking hours, the live whales have to swim in their fellow creatures' blood awaiting their fate.

An extremely disturbing aspect of the hunt is that it is not selective in any manner and it is not unusual for pregnant and young to be killed.

The Faroe Islanders have been taking Pilot whales (Grind) for over 400 years. In the past whales supplied an essential food. Now there is no need for the continuation of the slaughter of these magnificent creatures. Their supermarkets are packed with a wide variety of foods which you and I would expect to find in this country.

SAVE Report, vol. 1, no. 1, Glasgow: Society Against the Violation of the Environment, 1985

The whaling will stop, but only when it's no longer profitable to whale. The economics of whaling are not very hard to understand: essentially the businessmen who control whaling have two options, they can go after as many whales as possible until there aren't enough left to support the industry, in effect they would be mining a profitable vein; or, they can take just the surplus production for a sustainable yield, milking rather than mining the whales. It seems obvious that milking would make more sense than mining, but sometimes the obvious is wrong. The trouble is that whale numbers increase very slowly indeed – perhaps less than two per cent a year, so that if you go for a sustainable yield all the money you have got tied up in ships and crew will earn a very small return. As a businessman it makes most sense to take all the whales you can, and when all the whales are gone, you simply shift your profits into some other venture. It'll always pay to go after just one more whale. That is why whalers ignore calls to reduce the catch, that is why they break the rules whenever they feel like it. Sustainable whaling will never happen simply because money in the bank grows quicker than whales in the water.

Jeremy Cherfas, *Battle for the Whales*, Television Documentary, London: BBC, transmitted June 1986

The International Whaling Commission began functioning in 1948 for the purpose of rebuilding the whaling industry, which had been severely disrupted during World War II. It is dominated by the whaling industry, not by governments, and, although man has hunted whales as long as he has known them, nothing can match the carnage since the IWC has been in existence. Huge fleets abetted by sonar, helicopters, factory ships, explosive harpoons, and all such modern-day technologies have decimated the populations of the eight species of great whales until they are threatened with extinction. The whale killers – mainly Japan and the Soviet Union – blithely ignore the toothless sanctions adopted at each IWC meeting.

And the ultimate irony is that, while the slaughter goes on at the rate of one whale killed every twenty minutes, anything that these warm-blooded, air-breathing, milk-giving creatures provided to mankind can be duplicated from other sources.

Paul Watson, *Sea Shepherd, My Fight for Whales and Seals*, as told to Warren Rogers, London and New York: W. W. Norton, 1982

The International Whaling Commission on the outskirts of Cambridge is supposed to safeguard the world's whales. In the past few years the annual meetings of the I.W.C. have seen their own share of emotion and conflict. But in the beginning it was essentially a whalers' club. The whaling countries got together to divide up the spoils, and even today the I.W.C. has very little real power. Nations can object to any decision they don't like, and nothing, apart from public opinion, forces them to join. Also, it takes a three-quarters majority to alter any I.W.C. decision so change comes very slowly. For years the I.W.C. ignored the advice of its own scientists, who told them again and again that the whales were being exterminated. A moratorium, a temporary halt, did eventually get passed: ten years, and more than a quarter of a million whales after it was first suggested. But only because the conservationists drafted in a host of sympathetic countries to get the necessary majority. It took so long because the whalers were always able to say that there was no evidence that the whales were being over-exploited. And even today, the one thing we really know about whales, is how little we know about whales.

Jeremy Cherfas, *Battle for the Whales*, London: BBC, transmitted June 1986

S ince its inception a century and a half ago, commercial whaling has pursued a pattern of exploitation that has remained unfortunately aloof from biological knowledge. This sterile operational philosophy has produced an unbroken series of biological catastrophes. One by one the stocks of large whales have been depleted; population after population has been reduced to commercial and ecological insignificance . . . One by one the whale populations have disappeared, and the entire commercial whaling enterprise is in a state of collapse.

G. A. Bartholomew, 'The Relation of the Natural History of Whales to their Management', in *The Whale Problem*, ed. William E. Schevill, Cambridge, Mass.: Harvard University Press, 1974

S perm whale hunting in the Azores resumed in 1984 with a catch of 63 whales. In 1983, when the catch fell to 23, it was reported that the hunting would cease due to a lack of markets for the whale oil. The storage tanks of the last operating whaling station in the Azores, Armacoes Baleeiras Reunidas Lda, were full with the stockpiled oil production from 1981, '82, and '83.

In late 1983, the owner of the Pico station, Jose Christiano, found a buyer for his oil stocks, estimated to be around 1000 tons. In December, 1983 and June, 1984, the oil was shipped aboard the Portuguese tanker 'Angol' to Lisbon to the company of Gomes Severino, a dealer in fish and vegetable oils. Gomes Severino formerly supplied sperm oil to numerous EEC countries, but claimed that their last export to Europe was a sum of 435 tons in 1980 to the French firm of Daubruy in Dunkirk.

In February 1985, a further shipment of 240 tons of whale oil was sent from Pico to Lisbon. The Lisbon based pharmaceutical company, Antral Cipan admitted they had received 170 tons of whale oil from the shipment, which they had used in the fermentation process for antibiotic production. The company also acknowledged receiving 150 tons of oil in 1984.

Gomes Severino claimed that the rest of the oil was sold domestically but would not name any other company receiving it. Export statistics for Portugal for 1983, published by the OECD, reveal that 157 tons of 'marine mammal oil' was exported: 60 tons to the Netherlands and 97 tons to Spain. Sperm whales are the only marine mammal commercially exploited in Portugal.

One canoe and two motor launches operated in the Azores in 1984. The skipper of one launch, Antonio Jose, said that 'The oil from the 1981, '82 and '83 catches was sent to Lisbon and then sold clandestinely to another country where it is prohibited to import it.' The owner of the Pico station said in October, 1984 'Now we sell the oil to Rotterdam.' Antonio Avila de Melo, a Lisbon based fisheries scientist conducting research on Azorean sperm whaling since 1982 said 'Part of the oil is sent to a pharmaceutical factory in Lisbon and part is exported. They didn't tell me which country it was sent to.' A fourth person, a government official in the Azores, also stated that the oil was sent to Rotterdam.

The exports of sperm whale oil are in violation of the Convention of International Trade in Endangered Species (CITES) which Portugal joined in 1980. CITES prohibited trade in sperm whale products in 1981 and Portugal did not object to the listing. Although Portugal and the EEC have reached agreement on Portuguese accession to the Community, there has not been any agreement as yet for Portugal to abide by the EEC ban on whaling.

Portugal announced in 1983 that they intended to join the International Whaling Commission, but changed its mind apparently because a zero quota on sperm whales in the North Atlantic had already been established.

Dr. Fernando Cordosa, the assistant to the Minister of Fisheries in the Azores Regional Government stated in October, 1984, 'We don't officially know that products from the Azores whale hunt are being exported to countries which prohibit their import. If somebody complains, we will have to investigate.'

Nick Carter and Allan Thornton, *Pirate Whaling 1985, and a History of the Subversion of the International Whaling Regulations*, London: Environmental Investigation Agency, 1985

In *Porpoise, Dolphin and Small Whale Fisheries of the World*, Dr. Edward Mitchell writes: 'The U.S. Navy was asked to rid the coastal areas of killer whales.'

Mitchell cites a 1956 report: 'Last year VP-18 destroyed hundreds of killer whales with machine guns, rockets and depth charges. Before the Navy lent a hand, killer whales threatened to cut the Icelandic fish catch in half.'

Bourne wrote, in 1965, that the North Atlantic killer whale (orca, or blackfish) was often shot on sight by fishermen. The shooting of orcas occurs with varying intensity all over the world.

During 1973–1974, while filming killer whales off Vancouver Island, I awoke several mornings to the crackling of gunfire, only to watch whales quickly leaving the area. I was not surprised to come across a statistic in 1973 revealing that bullet holes had been found in sixty percent of all orcas captured and examined by scientists. And these were animals the gunshots had not killed.

Eric Hoyt, 'Orcinus Orca', *Oceans*, 55 (vol. 10, no. 4), San Francisco, July–August 1977

At the 1972 meeting of the International Whaling Commission, the United States delegation was trying to gain acceptance of a ten year moratorium on commercial whaling. The Scientific Committee of the I.W.C. recommended against the moratorium on the basis that further research was necessary; and that research required whaling. Russell Train, the U.S. Commissioner, said: 'Well, I can understand the need for more whales to study, but do you really need thirty-five thousand?' And Raymond Gamble, the senior British scientist, stroked his chin, smiled across the table, and said, 'Yes, lots more!'

Two million whales have been killed in the last fifty years. The industry and the scientists connected with the industry have had an opportunity to examine the corpses of two million whales and yet maintain a need for still more to study. We can pile up the tables of weights and lengths and ages and measures until it reaches the sky, but it won't get us an understanding of the living creature.

Joan McIntyre, 'Iceberg', in *Mind in the Waters*, New York: Scribner, 1974

The Americans are universally allowed to be the most resolute & expert in this Branch [the sperm-whale fishery]; for of the various species of whalemen which are known, the English, Dutch and other European nations, who pursue the Whale-Fishery, only kill a particular kind of bone-whale (the Right Whale) found in the Greenland and other seas, and as the attack on the other kinds (Sperm Whale and Humpback) requiring more dexterity and being attended with more danger, they do not attempt it. The American on the contrary successfully encounters every kind of whale & are the only people who kill the Sperm Whale.

Petition of Francis Rotch to the Right Honourable Lord Commissioner of His Majesty's Treasury [Lord North], *28th November, 1775*, Public Records Office, Colonial Office 5, vol. 146, p. 63, London

The history of whaling has been characterized by a progression from more valuable or more easily caught species to less attractive ones as stocks of the original targets were depleted.

K. Radway Allen, *Conservation and Management of Whales, Division of Marine Resources*, Seattle: University of Washington Press, 1980

The *Star of the East* was in the vicinity of the Falkland Islands and the lookout sighted a large Sperm Whale three miles away. Two boats were launched and in a short time one of the harpooners was enabled to spear the fish. The second boat attacked the whale but was upset by a lash of its tail and the men thrown into the

sea, one man being drowned, and another, James Bartley, having disappeared, could not be found. The whale was killed and in a few hours was lying by the ship's side and the crew were busy with axes and spades removing the blubber. Next morning they attached some tackle to the stomach which was hoisted on the deck. The sailors were startled by something in it which gave spasmodic signs of life, and inside was found the missing sailor doubled up and unconscious. He was laid on the deck and treated to a bath of sea water which soon revived him . . . He remained two weeks a raving lunatic . . . At the end of the third week he had entirely recovered from the shock and resumed his duties.

Ambrose John Wilson, *The Sign of the Prophet Jonah and its Modern Confirmation*, vol. 25, Princeton Theological Review, 1927

With a bump of the nose it could break your steering-oars, with a blow from the tail it could smash a fragile vessel to bits. But nothing of the sort happens, as long as you do not run a harpoon into the amiable visitor. The whale, if any surviving animal giant has, has little reason to deal lightly with the tiny human species, yet with all its tremendous body-strength it never touched our vessel nor even scratched loose a reed from the bundles. It made sure never to bump into us even in the pitch dark. At an arm's length it could suddenly come up, with the colossal head pointing straight for us, then it would bow head under and slide like a shadow right beneath our bundles to come up on our other side and resume the journey it had interrupted merely to pass by and say a friendly hello.

It is not everybody's fortune to have had bedside company with whales in their own free playground. But those of us who have, feel an urge to support the growing majority of mankind that demands that the tiny minority who threatens the remaining whale species with complete extinction for personal economic gains should be forced to leave the whales in peace until able to multiply for the benefit of future generations on this planet.

Thor Heyerdahl, 'The Friendly Whale', from *Whales*, ed. Greg Gatenby, Boston, Mass.: Little, Brown, 1983

It would appear that we are more willing to consider the possibility of other intelligences on distant planets than we are on our own.

Keith Howell, 'Consciousness of Whales', *Oceans*, 55 (vol. 10, no. 4), San Francisco, July–August 1977

The fireplace was inlaid with lapis lazuli at a cost of five dollars a square inch, the bar hand-rails were made of the finest whale-tooth ivory engraved with scenes from the *Iliad* and the *Odyssey* . . .

It had cost him [Onassis] four million dollars to convert the fifty-thousand-dollar 322-foot Canadian frigate to what ex-king Farouk called 'the last word in opulence', and another guest described as 'the crystallization of Ari's charm'. If the taste level of the *Christina* was at times dubious (Marcel Vertes' frescoes of the seasons on the dining-room panels depicted the family in allegorical scenes: Tina ice skating, Alexander and Christina picnicking on a summer's lawn) and some-times vulgar (bar stools covered with white whale foreskin: 'Madame, you are now sitting on the largest penis in the world,' Ari informed Greta Garbo), it was never cheap. Modern technology (radar, forty-two-line telephone and telex system, air-conditioning plant, operating theatre and X-ray machine, electronic tempera-ture control to ensure that the water in the swimming pool, the floor of which could be raised to deck level for dancing, and which was decorated with mosaic scenes from Greek mythology, remained a refreshing ten degrees below air temperature) threaded the ship like a nerve system. In addition to his own four-room suite on the bridgedeck, with its sunken blue Siena marble bathtub (a replica of one built for a Minoan king) and Venetian mirrored walls, there were nine luxury suites, each named after a Greek island (Ithaca being the one usually reserved for his very special guests of honour and occupied variously by Garbo, Callas and Jackie Kennedy).

'I don't think there is a man or woman on earth who would not be seduced by the sheer shameless narcissism of this boat,' said Richard Burton.

Peter Evans, *Ari, The Life and Times of Aristotle Socrates Onassis*, London: Jonathan Cape, 1986

B ut notwithstanding, although the dolphins so excel in gentleness and though they have a heart so much at one with men, the overweening Thracians and those who dwell in the city of Byzas hunt them with iron-hearted devices – surely wicked men and sinful . . . who would not spare their children or their fathers and would lightly slay their brothers born.

Oppian (fl. A.D. 200), *Halieutica*, trans. A. W. Mair, London/Cambridge, Mass.: Heinemann/Harvard University Press, 1928

A quarter of a million dolphins are annually killed by the tunafish industry. Dolphins often swim with tunafish and are used as net markers, and end up being crushed to death in these nets.

Only in the last twenty-five years have these industries used nets to catch tuna, before this they used hooks and lines, and the dolphins were safe. But since these were replaced by large nets, over eight million dolphins have been killed.

World Marine Life Observers, Newsletter, Essex, 1986

Dr. Max Kramer has apparently found the most acceptable explanation of dolphin locomotion efficiency in his experiments with pressure accommodation. Dr. Kramer produced a synthetic dolphin skin which imitates the surface flexion of the live dolphin so successfully that a small craft coated with the synthetic skin experienced a 60 per cent reduction in drag. A coating of such skin on the nuclear-powered submarine combined with the already employed streamlined shape of the dolphin, should decrease drag in a ratio similar to that of the experimental craft.

Emory W. Brown, Jnr, 'The Dolphins: Like an Arrow They Fly through the Sea', *U.S. Naval Institute Proceedings*, July 1965

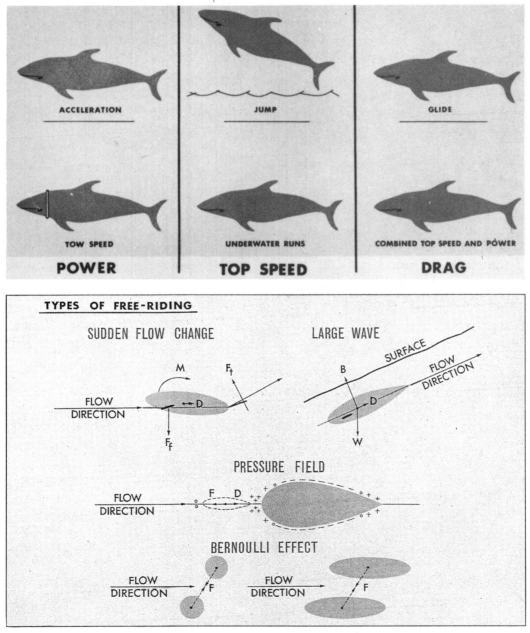

No sooner does man discover intelligence than he tries to involve it in his own stupidity.

Jacques Cousteau, *The Living Sea*, New York: Harper and Row, 1963

I n his bedroom near the dolphin tanks at the University of Hawaii, Steve Sipman 'could lay in bed at night and hear the dolphins making sounds. If they were distressed, you'd hear them making sounds. You get familiar with the dolphin's moods. Sometimes loneliness. Sometimes – restless. You know what their environment is. You know what they're missing. Sexual frustration. You understand this. The dolphins don't consider themselves anybody's pet.

'Nobody at the facility could avoid noticing the dolphin's ability to deal with abstract terms. They'll deal ten times better than we ever thought they could. And this is dangerous for them because, given the mood of man, they'll be made into aquatic servants, most likely. You know how the Navy worked to turn them into self-guided torpedoes. You say you'll train them, but training them, and even trying to talk with them, becomes a prelude to their destruction. And we say this is what makes the experiments worthwhile, it's what man has to accomplish. And, as it happens, I differ. I differ.'

Ted Crail, *Apetalk & Whalespeak: The Quest for Interspecies Communication*, Los Angeles/ Boston: J. P. Tarcher/Houghton Mifflin, 1981

[Steve Sipman was later to release the four dolphins from the Kewalo Basin Marine Mammal Research Laboratory, and return them to the Pacific.]

T he dolphin is an animal without malice, living to be a hundred years old, loving music and friendly to men.

Konrad of Megenberg, *Das Buch der Natur*, 1475

I t was a small whale, a Porpoise about eight feet long with lovely subtle curves glistening in the cold rain. It had been mutilated. Someone had hacked off its flukes for a souvenir. Two other people had carved their initials deeply into its side, and someone else had stuck a cigar butt in its blowhole. I removed the cigar and stood there a long time with feelings I cannot describe.

Roger S. Payne, quoted by Faith McNulty in 'Lord of the Fish', *New Yorker*, 6 August 1973

D olphins never abandon their young and if it happens that men catch a young dolphin, adult dolphins go to the extreme to save the imprisoned youngster. They come to the shore, allow the men to strike, hurt and even kill them.

On many occasions it was noticed that dolphins show human sensibilities and tenderness for other dolphins who are in trouble, hurt or sick. If a dolphin dies, others come together and help deliver the dead body to the shore . . . Witnesses tell us that on such an occasion, the dolphins weep and lament, showing human sensibility as they mourn the dead dolphin.

Dolphins are extremely sensitive to music and singing and they very much like young men who are musicians or singers. There is a story, too, of a lark which at the end of the warm season tried to escape the coming cold. By its merry singing it so enchanted a dolphin that the dolphin delivered it over the sea on its back.

Konrad Gesner (1551–1587), *History of Animals*, Zurich: Franco Furdi, 1586

D olphins of a species known as *Tursiops truncatus* crowd by Cape Hatteras, in the St. Lawrence, in huge schools from late autumn to early spring . . . As many as a hundred animals could be taken at a single haul. This industry continued into the present century, principally because of a very special kind of oil that can be extracted from the lower jaws of the *Tursiops*.

The oil is taken from the back end of the lower jaw on either side, and, when refined, was once valued as high as twenty dollars a gallon. It is extremely light and perfectly suited for oiling small watches and other delicate instruments. Secondly, the hides of these animals make very fine leather, and the blubber yields other oil of high grade.

Ivan T. Sanderson, *Follow the Whale*, London: Cassell, 1958

Turkish fishermen are shooting and trapping dolphins on a scale which dwarfs the more widely-publicised dolphin massacres carried out by the Japanese.

According to the People's Trust for Endangered Species, more than 900,000 dolphins have been killed in the last fifteen years. Most of them were melted down for their oil with the leftovers being turned into chicken meal. But there has been little demand for dolphin oil since the EEC banned imports of whale products (which include dolphins and porpoises).

Between the Soviet Union, Bulgaria, Romania and Turkey, the Black Sea hunt was taking 250,000 dolphins a year in the Thirties. Then the inevitable happened. The dolphins suffered such a drastic decline that, in 1969, the first three countries banned the bloodbath . . .

Nevertheless, the fishermen of Trabzon and other Turkish Black Sea ports have still been out in force all winter long, harrying the dolphins as they migrate westward along the coast.

Sunday Times, London: April 1982

The eyeballs of the Amazon river dolphin (*Inia geoffrensis*) long valued as amulets by believers in the Brazilian voodoo cult Macumba, are now in vogue as lucky charms among non-believers.

The eyeballs are sold openly in markets and tourist shops in Rio de Janeiro and other major cities. They can even be bought by mail order, or through the yellow pages of telephone books. When local conservationists posed as potential buyers, a dealer said he could supply them with 500 eyeballs within a week at a cost of between \$1·50 to \$3·00 per eye.

Other dolphin products, on sale in Brazil, are also in demand, especially dolphin oil, which is highly regarded as a lure for fish. In addition, dolphin vaginas are said to lure men to the women who carry them . . . River dolphins are found only in China, India and the Amazon Basin . . . The Amazon river dolphin has not been well studied and there are no population estimates for the species. Brazil bans the export of dolphins or parts of dolphins but trade within the country is uncontrolled.

Catherine Caulfield, 'When eyeballs of dolphins become part of the traders' brew', *New Scientist*, London: 5 December 1985

The mortality in dolphinaria of killer whales may be in the order of ten times that in the wild, and of bottlenose dolphins two or three times that in the wild. In other words, dolphins in captivity have their life expectancy reduced by ten years and, for an orca, it is reduced by twenty years or more.

Review made by Dr S. Innes under the direction of Professor David Lavigne, of the University of Guelph, Ontario on all mortality data for marine animals, prepared for the International Wildlife Coalition, 1985

The Ito Hot Springs Tourist Association in Shizuoka-Ken (about two hours by train from Tokyo) has started a campaign to promote the eating of dolphins by tourists. While dolphin-eating may be a tradition in Ito city, it is not in other parts of Japan. Between 2000 to 2500 dolphins are killed yearly, but the numbers are sure to increase. An Ito restaurant owner claims that dolphin meat is good for health, cheap and that people who eat dolphins live long lives. The same owner stated 'human health is more important than protecting animals and fish.'
World Animal Welfare Group, Newsletter, Essex: March 1986

LUNCHEON MENU

HOT SPECIALTIES
(all served with crudités vinaigrette)

Dolphin Creole	**5.50**
poached fillet of dolphin in a spicy Creole sauce with rice	
Coquille St. Jacques	**7.50**
sea scallops poached in wine and served with a cream sauce over rice	
Sauteed Chicken Livers	**4.50**
with onions, apples, and seasoned rice	
Charbroiled Steak	**10.50**
twelve ounces of prime U.S. sirloin cooked to order	

Restaurant menu from St Croix, US Virgin Islands

Hidden in the Annex to the International Whaling Commission Scientific Report (1987) are unsettling revelations on the level of kill of small cetaceans. The Scientific Committee estimates that 150,000 small cetaceans were killed in 1986 alone.

Far and away the worst offender is Mexico. It is estimated that the Mexican commercial tuna fish industry killed more than 100,000 dolphins last year. The US also contributes to the problem. Last year, the US tuna fleet killed more than 20,500 dolphins in the Eastern Tropical Pacific. US law prohibits killing of any more than this number . . .
International Dolphin Watch, Newsletter, no. 16, Humberside: North Ferriby, November 1987

No animal of the sea or land figures more frequently in the fanciful creations of the Greeks and Romans than the dolphin, king of the Mediterranean Sea. It is represented in their myths as an attribute, symbol, companion, and servitor of the mighty gods, who were themselves not ashamed to borrow its form . . .

It is not strange, then, that these motives entered even the scientific work of antiquity, and the dolphin was elevated into an ethical type of the animal world . . . to dream of this wonderful animal signified good . . .
Paul Biedermann, *Der Delphin in der dichtenden Phantasie und bildenden der Griechen und Römer*, Halle: Stadtgymnasium, 1881

[In the fourth century B.C., Bacchylides of Ceos described dolphins as 'sea people'.]

POSEIDON: It's greatly to the credit of you dolphins that you've always been kind to man. Long ago you caught up Ino's son after his fall with his mother from the Scironian cliffs, and carried him to the Isthmus. And now one of you has picked up this harper [Arion] from Methymna, and swum away with him to Taenarum, robes and harp and all, stopping those seamen from murdering him.

DOLPHIN: Don't be surprised, Poseidon, that we're kind to men. We were men ourselves, before we became fishes.

Lucian, *Dialogues of the Sea Gods*, trans. M. D. Macleod, London/Cambridge, Mass.: Heinemann/Harvard University Press, 1961

Dolphins are never aggressive toward human beings – not even in captivity . . . Even the so-called killer whale (the largest of all dolphins with a brain weighing almost 9 pounds), known for its healthy appetite for all types of animal protein, is, in captivity, friendly toward human beings. And yet the captive whale can hardly take a positive view of its situation. One wonders if this control of aggression can be a function of the large brain and whether it has been of importance for the survival of species.

Karl-Erik Fichtelius and Sverre Sjölander, *Man's Place: Intelligence in Whales, Dolphins and Humans*, London: Gollancz, 1973

In our experience killer whales do not appear dangerous to man. Tales of killer whale attacks on boats are hotly debated even when documented. In any case they are rare, and have never resulted in a human death. Antarctic scientists I have talked with, however, were surprised at our daring in photographing killer whales underwater or even from a canoe.

'The substance of the fear of orca in the Antarctic,' explains Price Lewis of the Science Foundation in Washington D.C. 'is that men working near the edge of the polar ice will be mistaken by predatory orcas for penguins (and bumped off) and divers in their wetsuits for seals.'

This belief goes back to 1911 and the oft-told account of Herbert Ponting, British photographer for Scott's last Antarctic expedition. While Ponting stood on a floe snapping pictures, orcas suddenly broke through two and a half feet setting him adrift. He barely escaped by hopping from one ice floe to the next.

Did the whales mistake Ponting's six foot dark shape for that of a seal? Were they merely exuberantly curious? Had Ponting fallen in, would they have finished him off? I suspect not – if the whales had time to realize their mistake. But even if Antarctic orcas are not man-eaters, curiosity or mistaken identity could perhaps be fatal to men visiting there because whales and men are not as familiar with one another as they are, for example, in the densely populated Northwest where natives have fished close to orcas for centuries. Still, in the north, there is a healthy respect for the animals' size and power.

Erich Hoyt, 'Orcinus Orca', *Oceans*, 55 (vol. 10, No. 4), San Francisco, July–August 1977

[The reputation of the orca as a 'killer' is recent, and may, like the reputation of the tiger, and leopard, turned man-eater, have been caused by man's encroachment upon the orca's habitat, and normal food supply, reduced by man's depredations.

Over-fishing caused the orcas to scavenge upon dead and bleeding whales tied for long periods to the sides of whaling ships. Thus did seamen call them 'killers', and hyenas of the sea. The killing pre-dated the orca's activities.]

I knew of no incident in which a Bottlenose dolphin had attacked and seriously injured a human. Indeed, it was widely accepted that even when provoked dolphins do not retaliate aggressively.

Unlike sharks, whose teeth are razor sharp and designed to slice through flesh and bone, Percy [a dolphin encountered off the coast of Cornwall] had conical interlocking teeth devised to grasp prey. None the less, if he so desired, we had no doubt he could break our limbs like matchsticks. He could also dispatch us by ramming us with his beak, which is the time-honoured method reported to be used by dolphins for killing sharks. It was therefore with some concern that we set out to film him.

We were fairly close in-shore and an adult couple swam out to see us. The lady was topless and when Percy approached her she shrieked. Then, to our utmost surprise, Percy butted her in the midriff and pushed her under the water. She came up choking . . .

I had already noticed that Percy had distinct preferences regarding people in the water and that he would completely ignore some swimmers, no matter how hard they tried to impose their company upon him. However, I had never seen him express his apparent disapproval of anyone so forcefully before.

Apart from a boat handler the only other passenger in the boat with us that day was Tricia Kirkman. She had acquired a wetsuit and was trying to pluck up courage to go into the water with Percy – despite the fact that she could not swim. When she saw what happened to the topless woman, who was obviously an extremely good swimmer, Tricia had to summon up every ounce of her courage to venture into the sea. I told her if she was quiet and gentle she would be all right.

She put on fins, mask and snorkel and slid very quietly over the side. Percy approached her and then turned upside down. Tricia grasped his fins as if they were outstretched arms. The dolphin very slowly towed her through the water. I quickly put a new film in my underwater camera, and when I got back into the sea, Tricia, who had been alone in the water with the dolphin, was about seven yards from the boat. As I swam towards them I saw one of those sights that burnt into my memory and left a permanent image. Tricia was floating on the surface with her arms straight down and her hands resting very lightly on Percy's head. The dolphin was swimming very slowly forwards so that the two of them were gliding through the water. The red colour of Tricia's wetsuit reflected from the surface of the water contrasted with her long black flowing hair. It was a picture of great beauty, peace and harmony, one of those incidents in life which last only briefly, yet are extremely significant. Here was a woman who could not swim floating across the deep sea, propelled by a wild dolphin.

During her entire stay in the water Percy never gave Tricia one moment's cause for alarm. When she was eventually hauled back into the Zodiac [inflatable] she sat on one of the tubes with her legs dangling in the water. As she did so Percy slid up from the depths, raised his head out of the water and rested it on Tricia's lap. She bent her head down and Percy rose higher to gently touch her face with the tip of his beak.

In 1974 I saw my son ride on a wild dolphin. In 1984 I saw a wild dolphin kiss a lady.

Horace Dobbs, *Tale of Two Dolphins*, London: Jonathan Cape, 1987

There are many instances of dolphins supposedly piloting ships into port. Some of the dolphins which were supposed to do this became so familiar that they earned names for themselves. The most famous of these was Pelorus Jack, a dolphin or, perhaps, a Pilot whale which, for thirty-two years up to 1914 used to meet ships in the Pelorus Channel, in the South Island of New Zealand, and escort them up narrow Marlborough Sound. During the last ten years of his life Pelorus Jack was a national institution, protected by law, and anyone who shot at or tried to harm him was liable for a fine of up to £100.

F. D. Ommanney, *Lost Leviathan*, London: Hutchinson, 1971

Is there any evidence that dolphins save drowning swimmers? There is.
    In 1945 the wife of a well-known trial attorney residing in Florida was saved

from drowning by a dolphin ('Saved by a Porpoise', *Natural History*, LVIII, 1949, 385–386). This woman had stepped into a sea with a strong undertow and was immediately dragged under. Just before losing consciousness, she remembers hoping that someone would push her ashore. 'With that, someone gave me a tremendous shove, and I landed on the beach, face down, too exhausted to turn over . . . when I did, no one was near, but in the water almost eighteen feet out a porpoise was leaping around, and a few feet beyond him another large fish was also leaping.'

In this case the porpoise was almost certainly a dolphin and the large fish a fishtail shark. A man who had observed the events from the other side of a fence told the rescued woman that this was the second time he had seen a drowning person saved by a 'porpoise'.

More recently, on the night of February 29, 1960, Mrs. Yvonne M. Bliss of Stuart fell from a boat off the east coast of Grand Bahama Island in the West Indies. 'After floating, swimming, shedding more clothing for what seemed an eternity, I saw a form in the water to the left of me . . . It touched the side of my hip and, thinking it must be a shark, I moved over to the right to try to get away from it . . . This change in my position was to my advantage as heretofore I was bucking across tide and the waves would wash over my head and I would swallow a great deal of water. This sea animal which I knew by this time must be a porpoise had guided me so that I was being carried with the tide.

'After another eternity and being thankful that my friend was keeping away the sharks and barracuda for which these waters are famous, the porpoise moved back of me and came around to my right side. I moved over to give room to my companion and later knew that had not the porpoise done this, I would have been going downstream to deeper and faster moving waters. The porpoise had guided me to the section where the water was the most shallow. Shortly I touched what felt like fish netting to my feet. It was seaweed and under that the glorious and most welcome bottom.

'As I turned toward shore, stumbling, losing balance, and saying a prayer of thanks, my rescuer took off like a streak on down the channel.'

Winthrop N. Kellogg, *Porpoises and Sonar*, Chicago: University of Chicago Press, 1961

A 23-year-old woman, Yvonne Vladislavich, who swam for 25 miles in the shark infested Indian Ocean after a shipwreck off Lourenço Marques, Mozambique, says that she owes her life to two dolphins. She was on a cabin cruiser when a wave overturned and sank the boat. Miss Vladislavich decided to swim toward land for help. She had cut her foot and she saw half a dozen sharks trailing her. As the sharks circled closer, she said, two dolphins appeared at her side. The dolphins protected her until she reached a buoy and climbed up on it. Three other passengers drowned.

New York Times, 10 September 1972

John Lilly wanted to make a film of a dolphin rescuing a human being in the water. So George [Hunt] gets in the water and pretends to be in distress. Sissy [a porpoise] comes over and rescues him by pushing him to the side. Lilly is filming this, but when he looks at the camera he finds the cap is still on the lens. So he takes the cap off the lens and sends George back into the water. When George pretends to be in distress again, Sissy beats him up.

Gregory Bateson, 'Observations of a Cetacean Community', in *Mind in the Waters*, ed. Joan McIntyre, New York: Scribner, 1974

Perhaps the water barrier has shut us away from a potentially communicative and jolly companion. Perhaps we have some things still to learn from the natural world around us before we turn to the far shores of space and whatever creatures may await us there. After all, the porpoise is a mammal. He shares with us an ancient way of birth and affectionate motherhood. His blood is warm, he breathes air as we do. We both bear in our bodies the superficial remnants of a common skeleton torn asunder for divergent purposes far back in the dim dawn of mammalian life. The porpoise has been superficially streamlined like a fish.

His are not, however, the cold-blooded ways of the true fishes. Far higher on the tree of life than fishes, the dolphin's paddles are made-over paws, rather than fins. He is an ever-constant reminder of the versatility of life and its willingness to pass through strange dimensions of experience. There are environmental worlds on earth every bit as weird as what we may imagine to revolve by far-off suns. It is our superficial familiarity with this planet that inhibits our appreciation of the unknown until a porpoise, rearing from a tank to say Three-Two-Three, re-creates for us the utter wonder of childhood . . . The mysteries surrounding the behaviour of the bottle-nosed porpoise, and even of man himself, are not things to be probed simply by the dissector's scalpel. They lie deeper. They involve the whole nature of the mind and its role in the universe.

We are forced to ask ourselves whether native intelligence in another form than man's might be as high, or even higher than his own, yet be marked by no material monuments as man has placed on earth. At first glance we are alien to this idea, because man is particularly a creature who has turned the tables on his environment so that he is now engrossed in shaping it, rather than being shaped by it.

It is difficult for us to visualize another kind of lonely, almost disembodied intelligence floating in the wavering green fairyland of the sea – an intelligence possibly near or comparable to our own . . . Hidden in their sleek bodies is an impressively elaborated instrument, the reason for whose appearance is a complete enigma.

Perhaps man has something to learn after all from fellow-creatures without the ability to drive harpoons through living flesh . . .

Loren Eiseley, 'The Long Loneliness', *American Scholar*, Winter 1960–61

News came through of yet another friendly wild dolphin – this time off Solva on the coast of Pembrokeshire. So I drove to the south-west corner of Wales where I met Simo – an adolescent male Bottlenose dolphin. Simo enchanted the inhabitants of Solva and the holidaymakers who swam out to see him and sometimes play with him.

Whilst staying in Solva I gave a film lecture on dolphins at the Harbour House Hotel. During the show I expounded my views on the beneficial effects dolphins had on people suffering from nervous depression. Shortly afterwards I was approached by the owner of the hotel who said that one of her guests, a personal friend, was being treated for depression at Oxford. She asked if I would take him out to see the dolphin. So, in the company of Tricia Kirkman, who was working with me on a film about Simo and was totally under the spell of the dolphin, we took the middle-aged man called Bill to see Simo.

Tricia told him of her experiences with Percy and Simo and how the dolphin wouldn't harm him if he got in the water. She also told him how she experienced a great feeling of what she described as 'Pure Love' coming from Simo when she was with him. Furthermore she explained how the dolphin reacted to what people felt inside. It didn't matter in physical terms whether they were fat or thin, rich or poor – if they were gentle and sensitive inside, the dolphin would respond accordingly. The dolphin would not judge them by human standards but the standards of an intelligent being without possessiveness but in harmony with its environment.

Simo had very distinct likes and dislikes when it came to people. There were some who got only fleeting attention. Others he would play with for as long as they had stamina to keep up the pace. Bill definitely fell into the second category. The dolphin loved him. And we watched the man change from being apprehensive, scared and withdrawn to a smiling joyous person who became totally involved with the dolphin and forgot everyone and everything around him.

'He blossomed – just like a sunflower,' said Tricia.

Bill was almost tearful when he described his experience and his feelings to his family when we returned to shore.

'Wouldn't it be lovely if we could have boatloads of sunflowers like Bill,' said Tricia. I agreed and made tentative plans to conduct a clinical trial and introduce more people like Bill to Simo. I decided to call the study 'Operation Sunflower'. But I was thwarted in my plans because both Simo and Percy disappeared without trace.

I have to admit that with more people in hospitals for the treatment of mental complaints than for any other single condition, success in the venture would have brought its own problems on me. The number of patients who could be treated would be extremely limited for a host of reasons – high amongst them being the sheer physical impossibility of placing large numbers of people in the proximity of wild dolphins.

But a possible solution to that problem came to me when Laurie Emberson's film about Percy, 'Eye of the Dolphin', was shown on television. His film was not about structured scientific experiments. It was an almost random record of the antics of a wild dolphin and the responses of a few of the humans who were fortunate enough to come into close contact with him. Yet an unprecedented number of people wrote to the BBC saying how uplifted they were by the film. On reflection I realised there had been a similar response to my own films – especially when they were shown in places like Belfast. Thus it occurred to me that it might be possible to capture the essential emotion-changing quality that dolphins have on film . . . and then re-create it with the aid of technology when and where we want to.

That is something we are going to attempt to find out in Project Sunflower.

Horace Dobbs, 'Dolphins – Can they dispel the blues?', *World Magazine*, London, May 1987

Whenever Amazon fishermen gather, someone has a porpoise story to tell. The fresh water, Amazon River porpoise (*Inia geoffroyensis*), known locally as *bouto* . . . is credited with many natural and supernatural powers.

They will tell you how a lone canoeist is sometimes relieved of his paddle and left adrift by a porpoise coming up from beneath the boat and carrying off the paddle in his mouth. However, this same capricious fellow is reported to have saved the lives of helpless persons whose boats have capsized, by pushing them ashore. None of the dreaded flesh-eating *piranhas* appear when the porpoise is present, for they themselves would be eaten.

In the realm of the supernatural, *boutos* are reported to come ashore in disguise during the many *fiestas* in the Amazon River villages. They reputedly enjoy the fun and dance with the girls, and many a fatherless child is credited to the presence of a *bouto* ashore during these festivals. A *bouto*'s eye properly prepared by a *paije* (witch doctor) gives its possessor unbelievable powers, ranging from success with the fair sex to the ability to hex one's enemies.

F. Bruce Lamb, 'The Fisherman's Porpoise', *Natural History*, LXIII, pp. 231–2, New York, 1954

Wild dolphins ride the bow. Then you see them making trails in the water like a skywriter – only these are feces trails, and it is carried out with such spectacle that you begin to suspect that it's a design they're making and they're very conscious of the design and of seeing how far they can go. For all I know, it's calligraphy done with feces. Because the mind of the dolphin is strange and it's busy. It's always busy. You watch dolphins in the sandy bottom and they're drawing in the sand.

Steve Sipman (University of Hawaii), cited in Ted Crail, *Apetalk & Whalespeak: The Quest for Interspecies Communication*, Los Angeles/Boston: J. P. Tarcher/Houghton Mifflin, 1981

When we looked at these sections [of dolphin brain] I suddenly realized that these resembled the human brain to the point where the unpractised eye could not tell the difference between the cortical layers of the human and those of the dolphin. The only significant difference was that the dolphin had a thicker layer number one on the outside of the cortex. From studies of the 11,000 microscopic sections made of these brains, Morgane, Jacobs and Yakovlev have been writing many scientific papers and are currently preparing an atlas of the dolphin brain.

Those results show that the dolphin's cell count is just as high per cubic millimeter as is that of the human. The material also shows that the connectivity –

i.e. the number of cells connected to one another – is the same as is that in the human brain. They have also shown that there are the same number of layers in the cortex of a dolphin as there are in that of a human.

In other words, this brain is as advanced as the human brain on a microscopic structural basis.

John Lilly, *The Mind of the Dolphin*, New York: Doubleday, 1967

The brain size of whales is much larger than that of humans. Their cerebral cortexes are as convoluted. They are at least as social as humans. Anthropologists believe that the development of human intelligence has been critically dependent upon these three factors: brain volume, brain convolutions, and social interactions among individuals. Here we find a class of animals where the three conditions leading to human intelligence may be exceeded, and in some cases greatly exceeded.

The Cetacea hold an important lesson for us. The lesson is not about whales and dolphins, but about ourselves. There is at least moderately convincing evidence that there is another class of intelligent beings on Earth beside ourselves. They have behaved benignly and in many cases affectionately toward us. We have systematically slaughtered them. Little reverence for life is evident in the whaling industry – underscoring a deep human failing . . . In warfare, man against man, it is common for each side to dehumanize the other so that there will be none of the natural misgivings that a human being has at slaughtering another . . .

Carl Sagan, *The Cosmic Connection*, New York: Doubleday, 1973

Dolphin societies are extraordinarily complex, and up to ten generations coexist at one time. If that were the case with man, Leonardo da Vinci, Faraday, and Einstein would still be alive . . . Could not the dolphin's brain contain an amount of information comparable in volume to the thousands of tons of books in our libraries?

Senator Hubert Humphrey, quoting the Russian delphinologist, Yabalkov, at the 1970 U.S. Senate hearings on the Marine Mammal Protection Act.

The subject of dolphin intelligence is a very controversial one amongst scientists. The fact that some of the best brains in the world are seriously debating the issue lends a certain credibility to the hypothesis that dolphins are in some way unique as a species. Professor Teizo Ogawa of the University of Tokyo describes the intelligence of whales and dolphins as follows: 'In the world of mammals there are two mountain peaks, one is Mount Homo Sapiens, and the other is Mount Cetacea'. But a major difficulty in comparing the intelligence of man with that of dolphins is the fact that we have evolved in two such different environments. The so-called 'environmental factor', which makes comparisons of intelligence even between different ethnic groups of men extremely difficult, becomes an almost impenetrable barrier when comparing men and dolphins . . .

Whales in the past have been treated simply as a resource to be husbanded and exploited for our benefit. Should we now establish a new category of animals, completely separate from man, but which are accorded intelligence, social structure and a consciousness on a par with that of man? If we can humble ourselves enough to accept this possibility, we may find that we are at the dawn of a new era of understanding what life is about.

Man through his history has devoted most of his energies to the provision of food, shelter and transport for himself and his family. Today, for instance, motor car assembly workers labour at producing the means of transport and are paid in money, which in turn enables them to buy food produced by farmers and fuel hacked out of the ground by coalminers. Man in other words has devoted his intelligence to adapting the environment to suit his needs. The majority have little time to play and enjoy themselves.

Cetaceans, on the other hand, instead of attempting to control their immediate surroundings, have themselves adapted through the process of evolution to harmonise with their environment. A dolphin lives in an ecosystem in which food is abundant. He has no need to construct a shelter. Unburdened by possessions, avarice must be unknown to him. With the open sea as a common heritage Cetaceans do not suffer the tensions of living in high rise blocks of flats, the resentments of the squalor in shanty towns, or the burning hatred of suppression in ghettos. Having no money with which one dolphin can exploit another, they have no problem with the corrupting influence of power. No one dolphin has a fortune whilst another suffers the misery of poverty, and no starving dolphin swims alongside a bloated glutton. Unspurred by the greed for land, no dolphin technology has needed to develop mustard gas, flame throwers, defoliants or any of the other hideous instruments of human warfare . . .

With no technology, no art, no scientific achievements, one might ask, for what purpose did the Cetaceans evolve their large cerebral cortex through the past ten million years?

One answer to that question might be that the dolphins have evolved in order to enjoy and revel in the pleasure of simply being alive, of being dolphins.

And when the day comes that we can communicate intelligently with dolphins, they may introduce us to the concept of survival without aggression, and the true joy of living, which at present eludes us. In that circumstance what they have to teach us would be infinitely more valuable than anything we could offer them in exchange.

Horace Dobbs, *Follow a Wild Dolphin*, London: Souvenir Press, 1977

The Greeks held that killing a dolphin was tantamount to killing a man, and it was punished with the same penalty as murder.

G. Brenner and G. Pilleri, *Dolphins in Ancient Art and Literature, Investigations into Cetacea*, vol. VIII, Berne: Brain Anatomy Institute, 1977

The hunting of Dolphins is immoral and that man can no more draw nigh the gods as a welcome sacrificer nor touch the altars with clean hands but pollutes those who share the same roof with him, whoso willingly devises destruction for Dolphins. For equally with human slaughter the gods abhor the deathly doom of the monarchs of the deep . . .

Oppian (fl. A.D. 200), *Halieutica*, trans. A. W. Mair, London/Cambridge, Mass.: Heinemann/Harvard University Press, 1928

Straightway, with all his finery on, he [Arion] leaped down into the waves . . . Thereupon they say (it sounds past credence) a dolphin did submit his arched back to the unusual weight; seated there Arion grasped his lyre and paid his fare in song, and with his chant he charmed the ocean waves. The gods see pious deeds: Jupiter received the dolphin among the constellations, and bade him have nine stars.

Ovid (43 B.C.–A.D. 17), *Fasti*, trans. Sir James George Frazer, London/Cambridge, Mass.: Heinemann/Harvard University Press, 1931

Considering that we live in a world so entirely different from the world in which whales dwell, and that most of us never see them at all; and considering that everything surrounding their lives is shrouded in almost complete ignorance, it is a little hard to understand just where an interest in whales arises. Well, all we need to know is that it does arise . . . Whales have recently become a symbol of the wild world. It has been absolutely fascinating for me to watch it happen. They tend to lodge in the hearts of people – sometimes they lodge crosswise where they stick for life.

Roger Payne, foreword to Stanley M. Minasian, Kenneth C. Balcomb III and Larry Foster, *The World's Whales, The Complete Illustrated Guide*, Washington DC: Smithsonian Books, 1984

I wasn't always sure if I was the observer out there or the observed. Maybe the whales took more notes on me than I did on them. You'd see the big eyeball looking at you, and there's no question that in some ways the whale is more aware than you and I.

Steve Sipman (University of Hawaii), cited in Ted Crail, *Apetalk & Whalespeak: The Quest for Interspecies Communication*, Los Angeles/Boston: J. P. Tarcher/Houghton Mifflin, 1981

The sperm whale brain structure is such that this can be said to be a thinking animal capable of displaying high intellectual abilities.

Dr. A. A. Berzin, *The Sperm Whale*, National Marine Fisheries Service, Washington DC, 1972

This high and mighty God-like dignity inherent in the brow is so immensely amplified, that gazing on it . . . you feel the Deity and the dread powers more forcibly than in beholding any other living object in living nature.

Herman Melville, *Moby-Dick, or, The Whale*, New York: Harper and Brothers, 1851

The sovereign'st thing on earth Was parmaceti for an inward bruise.

William Shakespeare, *King Henry the Fourth, Part One*, Act I, Scene III

O ye whales, and all that move in the waters . . . 'Benedicite', *Book of Common Prayer*

Acknowledgments
and Index

Picture Credits

The author and the publishers would like to thank the following for their kind permission to reproduce illustrations: the University of Alaska (pp. 65 *top*, 148 *top right*); John Arsenault, University of Rhode Island (p. 13 *bottom*); Christopher Ash, Macmillan (pp. 57 *top*, 58 *bottom*, 60 *all*); Barnaby Picture Library (pp. 81 *bottom right*, 94 *bottom*, 141); Bavaria Verlag (p. 61); BBC Hulton Picture Library (pp. 63 *all*, 65 *bottom right and left*, 68 *top and bottom*, 70 *top and bottom*, 71 *top and bottom*, 72, 73 *top and bottom*, 74 *all*, 75 *top and bottom*, 76 *all*, 77 *all*, 79 *all except lower middle right*, 80 *all*, 81 *top right and left, middle and bottom left*, 83 *top*, 84 *top*, 142 *left*, 144 *bottom*, 145 *top left and right*); Joachim Blauel, Artothek (p. 87 *bottom*); Ann Brayton, University of Rhode Island (p. 15 *top*); Malcolm Brenner, © 1978 'Eyes Open' (p. 1); J. & S. Brownlie (p. 82); Reidar Brusell (p. 140 *left and right*); Michael Bryden (p. 178); Bureau of Naval Weapons and the Office of Naval Research, USA (pp. 167 *top and bottom*); Michael Calvert (p. 25); Cetacean Research Unit (pp. 16 *top*, 127); Rosemary Chastney, Ocean Images Inc (pp. 24 *top*, 35, 36 *bottom*, 47 *top*, 99 *top*); T. Collignon (p. 53); the Cousteau Society (pp. 2, 14 *top*, 28 *top*); Paulo Curto, Image Bank (cover and p. 95); Daily Telegraph Colour Library (pp. 8, 103); Horace Dobbs (p. 89); Euan K. Dunn (p. 180); Graeme Ellis, Nicklin Associates Ltd (pp. 22 *bottom*, 37 *bottom*); Richard Ellis (p. 28 *bottom*); Frank Essapian (p. 30 *bottom*); Jeff Foott, Survival Anglia (p. 18); D. E. Gaskin (pp. 57 *bottom*, 59 *top*); Al Giddings, Ocean Images Inc (pp. 11, 14 *bottom*, 15 *bottom*, 34, 37 *top*, 41, 44 *bottom*, 85, 88, 94 *top*, 99 *bottom*, 104, 105, 106, 107, 108, 109, 110, 182); François Gohier, Ardea London Ltd (pp. 7, 12 *top*, 86); William L. High (p. 166); Bob Hooper (p. 100 *top left*); James Hudnall (p. 42); Motoi Ichihara, Gyosei (pp. 20–1, 51, 55, 56 *top*) and 'Nankyokukai', Iwanami Shoten (Pacific Press Agency) (pp. 12 *bottom*, 31, 33, 48–9, 54 *top and bottom*); Jacana Agence de Presse (p. 17); Japan Whaling Association (p. 156); Winthrop N. Kellogg & Charles E. Rice (p. 90); Kendall Whaling Museum (pp. 62 *top*, 79 *lower middle right*, 144 *top left and right*, 153, 157); the Keystone Collection (p. 64); Tony Korody/SIGMA, John Hillelson Agency (p. 100 *bottom*); Frank W. Lane (p. 52); Zig Leszcynski, Oxford Scientific Films (p. 50); Kenneth E. Lucas (p. 27 *bottom*); Simon McBride (p. 170); A. R. Martin, Oxford Scientific Films (pp. 56 *bottom*, 83 *bottom*); Mary Evans Picture Library (pp. 66 *top and bottom*, 67 *top and bottom right*, 145 *bottom*, 148 *top left*); Pat Morris, Ardea London Ltd (p. 101 *top*); Tsuneo Nakamura (pp. 22 *top*, 39, 43 *top and bottom*, 44 *top*, 45, 133, 134); NASA (p. 158 *top and bottom*); Flip Nicklin, Nicklin Associates Ltd (pp. 10 *top*, 19, 23, 27 *top*, 38, 46, 93, 102, 112) and National Geographic © 1986 (p. 32); Peter

Parks, Oxford Scientific Films (p. 29); Roger Payne, Long Term Research Institute (p. 16 *bottom*); Robert L. Pitman (p. 124); Reader's Digest Association (p. 9); L. T. Rhodes, Oxford Scientific Films (p. 36); R. B. Robertson (pp. 57 *middle*, 58 *top*, 59 *bottom*, 62 *bottom*, 84 *bottom*); Ann Ronan Picture Library (pp. 67 *bottom left*, 69); Jennifer C. Rowley, Town Docks Museum, Hull (p. 148 *bottom*); Alfred Saunders (p. 84 *middle*); Sea World in association with Harcourt Brace Jovanovich (pp. 13 *top*, 26, 30 *top*, 92, 100 *top right*); Unieboek B.V. (p. 135); George L. Small, Associate Professor of Geography at the College of Staten Island, City University of New York (p. 136); Robert Stenuit (pp. 10 *bottom*, 91 *bottom*); Ronn Storro-Patterson (p. 40); Bob Talbot © 1986 (p. 174); Allen Thornton, Environmental Investigation Agency (p. 159); Norman Tomalin, Bruce Coleman Agency (p. 101 *bottom*, 169); Whaling Film Company (pp. 164 *top and bottom*); F. G. Woods (p. 24 *bottom*); Dave Woodward, University of Rhode Island (p. 47 *bottom*); Adam Woolfitt, Susan Griggs Agency (p. 6); Bernd and Melany Wursig, courtesy of the Whale Conservation Society (p. 114); Kazuo Yamamura (pp. 97 *top and bottom*, 98 *bottom*).

Acknowledgments

I would like to thank the copyright holders for permission to reproduce the material quoted in the section 'On the Nature of Whales', the sources of which are given beneath each extract. In addition, I am grateful for the generous help of Patricia Warhol of the American Cetacean Society; American Institute of Biological Sciences; Ken Andrews; Su Gooders of Ardea London Ltd; Desmond Elliot of Arlington Books; Joan Ball; Sal Shuel of BAPLA; Gregory Bateson; Andrew Mead and Susan Wookey of the BBC Hulton Picture Library; Amanda Barrett of the BBC Wildlife Unit; Martin Beck; Tony Bennett; Guy and Phoebe Bentinck; Jordan Bojilov; Margaret Bowden; John Bradshaw, Curator of Museums and Art Galleries, Kingston upon Hull; Malcolm Brenner; Mrs A. Oliver of the British Horological Institute; Polly Appleyard and Frank Wray of the British Library Document Supply Centre, Boston Spa; Emory W. Brown; Reidar Brusell; Paul Budker; Burmah-Castrol (UK) Ltd; Jerome Burne; Ken Campbell; Cathie Arrington, Ian Craig, Tony Colwell, Annelise Evans, Tom Maschler, Mon Mohan, Polly Samson, Elizabeth Smith and Hilary Turner at Jonathan Cape; Catherine Caulfield; Ned Chaillet; Jeremy Cherfas; Arthur C. Clarke; Robert Clarke; Robin Bamford, Harry Hawthorne and Dave Worth of Colour World, Plymouth; Anne-Marie Cousteau of the Cousteau Society; Neil Cunningham; Anthea Morton-Saner of Curtis Brown Ltd; David Day; Horace Dobbs; Simon Drake; John L. Dreher; Paul Addison of Edinburgh University, Department of History; Peregrine Eliot; Richard Ellis; Nick Carter, Jennifer Gibson and Allan Thornton of the Environmental Investigation Agency; European Space Agency; Lesley Fairbairn; Seiji Ohsumi of the Far Seas Fisheries Research Laboratory; Karl-Erik Fichtelius and Sverre Sjölander; Bob Flag; Peter Forbes; Stuart M. Frank; Greg Gatenby; Jacques Graven; Jeff Canin and Philip McNab of Greenpeace; Patrick Gribbin; Shingo Miyake of Gyosei; Leslie Harfoot; Selina Hastings; David Henderson, Assistant Keeper of Natural History, City of Dundee District Council; Jane Hill; Richard Horder; Takae Horton; Roy Hutchins; Motoi Ichihara; Togo Igawa; Ivan Illich; Jo Whiteman of Image Bank; Mary P. Wilkinson of the Imperial War Museum; Institute of Oceanographic Sciences; Hiroshi Kato; Vanessa Kelly; Tricia Kirkman of International Dolphin Watch; Morikuni Itabashi; Ruth I. Johns; John Joyce; Lutz Kroth; Ako Kunikida; Robert Lenkiewicz; Hilary Lewis; Kate Wilton of Liskeard Public Library; Tony Lister; Chris Bray, Cherry Bungay, David Campkin, Gilly Hancox, Andrew Lilley, David Salt and Pauline Thompson of Logo Design; Ellie Dorsey and Roger Payne of the Long Term Research Institute, Lincoln, Massachusetts; Barry Lopez; Helga Low;

Tim Lund; Joan McIntyre; Ruth McKenzie; Jonangus Mackay; Cilla Course, Tony Davies and Allen Varley of the Marine Biology Association, Plymouth; Scott F. Marion; Michael Marten; Juliet Duff of the Mary Evans Picture Library; Peter Matthieson; John May; Bora Merdsoy; Stanley Minasian; George Morley; Farley Mowat; Tsuneo Nakamura; J. E. Hill of the Natural History Museum; Cathy Martin of the Natural History Museum Library; Andrea Caunter and Paul Huxham of Nexus Colour Laboratory; Rick Geissler and Flip Nicklin of Nicklin Associates; Jim Nollman; Rosemary Chastney and Al Giddings of Ocean Images; Brian Servis of Optikos; Sandra Berry and Catherine Mason of Oxford Scientific Films; Shigeru Ueki of the Pacific Press Agency; Jean Parkin; David Pilbeam; Liz Nash and Michael Sewell of the Polytechnic Bookshop, Plymouth; PSI (Professional Scuba Inspectors), Washington; Quicksilver; Russ Aisthorpe of RMA Recording; Frank D. Robson; Ann Ronan of Ann Ronan Picture Library; Jennifer C. Rowley; Carl Sagan; Victor B. Scheffer; Neiti von der Schulenburg; Paul Watson of the Sea Shepherd Conservation Society; Amanda Sebestyen; Diana Senior; Diana Serpell; Ann Seymour; Steve Sipman; George Small, Associate Professor of Geography at the College of Staten Island, City University of New York; Valentine Abdy of the Smithsonian Institution; Linda Sommer; Ann Spurgeon; Ronn Storro-Patterson; Sue Harrison of Survival Anglia; Dr Oliver Taplin; Robert Temple; Rosemary A. Thurber; Ann McGrath of the Thoreau Lyceum, Concord, Massachusetts; Teresa Topolski; Unieboek B.V., Holland; United States Naval Institute; Peter Warshall; Lyall Watson; Paul Watson; Alan R. Torres of the Whale Centre, Oakland, USA; Kieran Mulvaney and Sean R. White of the Whale Conservation Society; Martin Wilkinson; China Williams; Elizabeth Williams; Dave Burrus of the World Animal Welfare Group; Richard Worthy; Kazuo Yamamura; John Williams of Youldens. *Sine qua non*. The publishers and I have made strenuous efforts to obtain necessary permissions with reference to copyright material, both illustrative and quoted, but there are some owners we have been unable to trace. If they would write to us, we shall be pleased to acknowledge them in any future edition.

Index

Whale Nation
First published 1988
Reprinted 1988 (twice)
Copyright © 1988 by Heathcote Williams

Jonathan Cape Ltd, 32 Bedford Square, London WC1B 3SG

A CIP catalogue record for this book
is available from the British Library.

ISBN 0 224 02555 4
0 224 02569 4 (pbk)

Printed in Italy by New Interlitho SpA, Milan